P9-DFS-902

WHAT IF?

Other Books by the Authors

ANNE BERNAYS

Professor Romeo
The Address Book
The School Book
Growing Up Rich
The First to Know
Prudence, Indeed
The New York Ride
Short Pleasures

PAMELA PAINTER

Getting to Know the Weather

WHAT IF?

Writing Exercises for
Fiction Writers

ANNE BERNAYS   PAMELA PAINTER

HarperCollins*Publishers*

Grateful acknowledgment is made to the following for permission to quote
from copyrighted material:

Excerpt from *Memento Mori*; by Muriel Spark, copyright 1958. Reprinted by
permission of Georges Borchardt, Inc., and the Author.

"My Pet" and "Total Recall" © 1990 by Alison Lurie

"Magnifying Conflict," "The Five-Highlighter Exercise," and "Cutting to the
Bone" © 1990 by David Ray

WHAT IF? Copyright © 1990 by Anne Bernays and Pamela Painter. *All rights
reserved*. Printed in the United States of America. No part of this book may
be used or reproduced in any manner whatsoever without written permission
except in the case of brief quotations embodied in critical articles and re-
views. For information address HarperCollins Publishers, 10 East 53rd Street,
New York, NY 10022.

Designed by Joan Greenfield

Library of Congress Cataloging-in-Publication Data
Bernays, Anne.
    What if? : writing exercises for fiction writers/Anne Bernays, Pamela
Painter.—1st ed.
       p. cm.
    ISBN 0-06-270038-3
    1. English language—Rhetoric—Problems, exercises, etc. 2. Fiction—
Technique—Problems, exercises, etc. 3. Creative writing—Problems, exer-
cises, etc. I. Painter, Pamela. II. Title.
PE1413.B47   1990
808'.066813—dc20   89-46518

90 91 92 93 94 CG/HC 10 9 8 7 6 5 4 3 2 1

To Our Students

CONTENTS

IV: PERSPECTIVE AND POINT OF VIEW   59

V: DIALOGUE   73

VI: PLOT   91

X: MECHANICS 167

XI: GAMES 205

ACKNOWLEDGMENTS

My husband, Justin Kaplan, for his editorial help and emotional support; Robie Macauley, for his sharp editorial eye. My daughter, Hester Kaplan, for evaluating many of these exercises. My agent, Gina Maccoby, for her patience and judgment; and our editor, Rick Kot, for his encouragement and enthusiasm.

ANNE BERNAYS

For all the same reasons, my thanks to Justin Kaplan and Anne Brashler; my agent, Roberta Pryor, and our editor, Rick Kot. Special thanks to my husband, Robie Macauley, for his companionable and instructive presence in the world of fiction, and to friends who contributed exercises from their own experience as teachers and writers.

PAMELA PAINTER

INTRODUCTION

.

ANNE BERNAYS: To be a good writer you must know how to do two very different things—write like a writer and think like one.

Writing like a writer means having absolute control over your material and your tools. Writing like a writer means, for instance, knowing when to use dialogue and when to summarize discourse, learning how to use adjectives and adverbs, and being able to name characters and anchor them in real time and space.

Thinking like a writer is more complex because it involves the unconscious. You can rely just so much on your five senses; after that you must exploit your curiosity, imagination, and capacity for skepticism—which is not to be confused with cynicism. Skepticism obliges you to look beneath the obvious to get at the true "meaning" of, say, a smile, a crying jag, a burst of anger. We have included exercises that ask the student to assume the opposite gender, to search for a subtext, to supply more than one reason for why certain events happen—in other words, to enhance that intuitive quality of mind possessed by all good writers of fiction.

PAMELA PAINTER: The exercises in *What If?* are meant to set something in motion. Each exercise is designed to help you to think in new ways, to discover your own material, to enrich the texture and language of your fiction, and to move steadily toward final meaning. And coming full circle, to help you begin again.

No matter how widely published, a writer always needs to begin again. We hope this book will be useful for people who have begun to publish and for those who have never written a word of fiction, for those writers working alone or in a writing group, as well as for writers teaching workshops or classes.

BERNAYS: "Can you *really* teach people how to write?" This is a question I've been asked more than any other. Beneath it is the implication that being able to write well is a divine gift—either you have it or you don't and no amount of schooling is going to make any difference. Obviously I don't agree or I wouldn't have been conducting writing workshops for so long. Besides, I think the question should be changed to "Can you really de-mystify the process of making up stories and writing them down?" While I frankly admit that I have no idea where the *ultimate* source of inspiration resides, I do insist that by breaking down the writing of fiction into its smallest—and most manageable—components you can learn how to write a singular story or even a novel. At the very least, you will feel far more at ease with written prose and will experience the joy of saying exactly what you want to say the way you want to say it.

PAINTER: Writing exercises have long been a part of the learning process for new and established writers. A good many entries in the published notebooks of writers such as Chekhov, Flaubert, Hemingway, Fitzgerald, and Maugham among others, are unlabeled writing exercises—exercises that grew out of analyzing or talking about what these authors were reading at the time. And many entries are tributes to those writers who had shown them by written example how something worked in fiction. Fitzgerald speaks of a "trick" he and Hemingway learned from Conrad (p. 212). John Gardner says of writing that it is a matter of "catching on." In *The Art of Fiction*, he says of exercises, "When the beginning writer deals with some particular, small problem, such as a description of a setting, description of a character, or a brief dialogue that has some definite purpose, the quality of the work approaches the professional." And eventually, for writers who are persistent, the exercises you do here will strengthen your writing as a whole.

BERNAYS: It's quite possible for someone to be a marvelous storyteller—so long as he doesn't have to write it down. Then there is the person who knows how to form moderately competent sentences, paragraphs, even pages, but has nothing fresh to say.

The exercises in this book will help the serious student sharpen her skills—at both thinking and writing like a writer. The raconteur will be able, at last, to write his story, and the competent composer will to come up with fresh and original ideas.

PAINTER: With practice and more practice. Just as every singer, visual artist, dancer, and composer must constantly practice his craft, the writer too must practice. Even though we use language every day in talking, writing letters, or writing notes to fill up the gas tank, or sometimes in our jobs writing memos, ad copy, or newspaper articles, this does not mean that we can forgo the practice required in other arts. Practice and persistence are also crucial to a writer. Learn to throw away the flawed sentence, to recast a weak character without feeling a sense of failure. You are growing by making these evaluations of your work. You are practicing the writer's craft.

BERNAYS: If the writer's engine is persistence, then her fuel is imagination; unlike real fuel, we have an endless supply of it and it costs nothing. Imagination is there in all of us, waiting to be released.

PAINTER: I became a believer in exercises when I did one for the first time in a writing workshop taught by Tom Bracken, a cofounder of *Storyquarterly.* Bracken gave us disparate elements to combine and weave into a story: banjo music, a penny, and an arresting photograph of two eyes peering through the grainy slats of a boarded-up window. Suddenly, for me, these things were transformed into a story about a lonely teenage girl sitting on an orange crate in a country store. She has a penny under her shoe—and knows that only the boy watching her through the boarded-up window has seen her slide it there. Even using the same details, we were amazed at how our stories were totally different from one another. But, of course, because each individual imagination—and voice and vision—used these details in a unique, personal way.

Since that time, I have worked with all kinds of exercises. Some are created as a result of reading the work of another writer—I think I will always ask of a particularly effective beginning: what has been set in motion, and how? Other exercises simply appeared out of thin air: "What if?" And others grew out of class discussion as when my student Ben Slomoff asked a question that suddenly illuminated everything: "You mean it's as if every story has its own history?" Yes, yes—that's it. And an exercise was born to convey just that to every class that followed.

BERNAYS: The exercises in this book represent the most successful examples of more than a hundred exercises used by both of us in over twenty-five years (combined) teaching at Harvard, Emerson, Vermont, Holy Cross, and the University of Massachusetts. Each exercise isolates a particular element of fiction, such as dialogue, characterization, subtext, and so on. In some cases, there's a two-page limit (approximately 550 words). This obliges the student to be clear, concise, and direct; to avoid long-windedness and straying from the point. I've found that whenever a student has gone much beyond the limit, the work turns fuzzy and boring. (In our minds boring is what you must never be as a writer. It's better to turn out prose that is rough than to put your reader to sleep.)

PAINTER: Although the table of contents is organized and ordered around the basic elements of writing fiction, there is no reason to follow this format. (And we made some discoveries while shaping the table of contents. We found that both of us believed in "character-driven" stories as opposed to "plot-driven" stories when we realized that we'd left "plot" as a distinct category out of our first draft.) In addition, these exercises are not organized in terms of their difficulty, and within each category you will find that some are easier to do than others.

We hope you will return again and again to various sections of *What If?*—combining and rearranging the exercises so that they lead you into your own limitless well of material and help you explore methods for realizing your potential as a writer. We also hope that you will use the writers whose work we have cited in our examples as a kind of organic reading list. Buy their books and read them; study specific passages, write in the margins, type out their sentences. Absorbing the work of great writers is the best education of all.

Interviewer: How do you describe the perfect state in which you can write from early morning into the afternoon?

One must be pitiless about this matter of "mood." In a sense, the writing will create the mood. If art is, as I believe it to be, a genuinely transcendental function—a means by which we rise out of limited, parochial states of mind—then it should not matter very much what states of mind or emotion we are in. Generally I've found this to be true: I have forced myself to begin writing when I've been utterly exhausted, when I've felt my soul as thin as a playing card, when nothing has seemed worth enduring for another five minutes . . . and somehow the activity of writing changes everything.

JOYCE CAROL OATES, *Paris Review* interview

WHAT IF?

I: BEGINNINGS

First sentences are doors to worlds.   —URSULA K. LE GUIN

NEW WRITERS OFTEN FIND BEGINNINGS DIFFICULT—WHETHER they're starting a story or a novel—because they take the word "beginning" too literally. They cast around for the "beginning" of a story—forgetting that beginnings rarely have the necessary ingredients for trouble, for conflict, or for complication. Your story can begin with dialogue, narrative summary, description, whatever, but it must begin *in medias res,* in the middle of things. You must resist the temptation to give the reader too lengthy an explanation as to how things got to this point. Remember, you are trying to hook the reader's attention, to pull the reader into your story so that he won't wonder, *What's on television tonight?*

Another stumbling block to beginning a story is that new writers think they have to know where their story is going and how it will end—before they begin. Not true. Flannery O'Connor says, "If you start with a real personality, a real character, then something is bound to happen; and you don't have to know what before you begin. In fact, it may be better if you don't know what before you begin. You ought to be able to discover something from your stories. If you don't, probably nobody else will."

The following exercises are designed to encourage you to think about real characters who are involved in situations that are already under way—situations that are starting to unravel because of, or in spite of, the desires and actions of their beleaguered characters. Don't worry about middles or endings yet. Just give yourself over to setting stories in motion—you will soon know which stories capture your imagination and seem unstoppable, which stories demand to be finished. Till that time, begin and begin and begin.

1

FIRST SENTENCES: BEGINNING IN THE MIDDLE

In a *Paris Review* interview, Angus Wilson says, "Plays and short stories are similar in that both start when all but the action is finished." This goes along with Horace's injunction to begin the story *in medias res*—in the middle of things.

Yet, beginners' stories often meander for three or four pages before the story begins to rear its head. One day, out of curiosity we decided to examine the first lines of stories in big and little magazines, story collections, and anthologies. We discovered that many *first sentences* put the reader in the middle of things. That exploration became the basis for this first exercise.

THE EXERCISE

Consider how many of the opening lines below pull you into the center of the story. What do you know about the story—situation, characters, geography, setting, class, education, potential conflict, etc.—from reading the titles and the following opening lines? What decisions has the author already made about point of view, distance, setting, tone, etc.? Notice how many of the titles are directly related to the first line of the text.

"The Lady with the Dog"   Anton Chekhov
They were saying a new face had been seen on the esplanade: a lady with a pet dog.

"Gesturing"   John Updike
She told him with a little gesture he had never seen her use before.

"Exchange Value"   CHARLES JOHNSON
Me and my brother Loftis came in by the old lady's window.

"The Remission"   MAVIS GALLANT
When it became clear that Alec Webb was far more ill than
anyone had cared to tell him, he tore up his English life and
came down to die on the Riviera.

"The Lost Cottage"   DAVID LEAVITT
The Dempson family had spent the last half of June in a little
rented cottage called "Under the Weather," near Hyannis,
every summer for twenty-six years, and this year, Lydia
Dempson told her son, Mark, was to be no exception.

"Medley"   TONI CADE BAMBARA
I could tell the minute I got in the door and dropped my bag,
I wasn't staying.

"The Winter Father"   ANDRÉ DUBUS
The Jackman's marriage had been adulterous and violent, but
in its last days they became a couple again, as they might have
if one of them were slowly dying.

"A School Story"   WILLIAM TREVOR
Every night after lights out in the dormitory there was a cer-
emonial story-telling.

"Cathedral"   RAYMOND CARVER
This blind man, an old friend of my wife's, he was on his way
to spend the night.

"Forgiveness in Families"   ALICE MUNRO
I've often thought, suppose I had to go to a psychiatrist, and
he would want to know about my family background, naturally, so I would have to start telling him about my brother,
and he wouldn't even wait till I was finished, would he, the
psychiatrist, he'd commit me.

"Appaloosa"   SHARON SHEEHE STARK
My father's girl friend's name was Delores and my mother
went by Dusie because she was one.

4

"The Handsomest Drowned Man in the World"
GABRIEL GARCÍA MÁRQUEZ
The first children who saw the dark and slinky bulge approaching through the sea let themselves think it was an enemy ship.

"Nickel a Throw"   W. D. WETHERELL
These are the things Gooden sees from his perch eight feet above the dunking tub at the Dixford Congregational Church's Charity bazaar.

"Inventing the Abbots"   SUE MILLER
Lloyd Abbot wasn't the richest man in our town, but he had, in his daughters, a vehicle for displaying his wealth that some of the richer men didn't have.

"Judgment"   KATE WHEELER
When Mayland Thompson dies he wants to be buried with the body of a twelve-year-old girl.

"Covering Home"   JOSEPH MAIOLO
Coach discovered Danny's arm when Danny's parents were splitting up at the beginning of the season.

"The Blue Men"   JOY WILLIAMS
Bomber Boyd, age thirteen, told his new acquaintances that summer that his father had been executed by the state of Florida for the murder of a Sheriff's deputy and his drug-sniffing German shepherd.

Now, write five of your own opening lines for five different stories. When you read, look for opening lines that immediately pull the reader into the story. And if you keep a journal or notebook, consider starting a new section and adding one first sentence a day—for the rest of your life.

THE OBJECTIVE

To get into the habit of beginning your stories in the middle of things. Because you are not obligated to finish these stories, this exercise lowers the emotional stakes and helps to shake up and surprise the imagination.

STUDENT EXAMPLES

She was trying to tell the joke right but it was his joke and she had to keep checking with him.

FRANCES LEFKOWITZ

I don't know who found me, or why I was left in a dumpster, but there was one piece of lore about my rescue that was not forgotten and that they made sure to hand down to me: written on my chest in navy blue Magic Marker, my original owner had put the word "Gem," and that is my real and only name.

BRIGID CLARK

By the time I was ten I had concluded that death was just a matter of moving furniture.

AMANDA CLAIBORNE, "Jemma"

My mother explained what sex was the day after I first had it.

CHRISTY VELADOTA

At Saint Boniface, on the first day of school, Mrs. Riordan found her fourth grade class was nothing more than Sister Mary's third grade from the year before, with one exception: a quiet boy with eyes the color of water, who occupied the front row window seat the way a vacuum takes up space.

BRIDGET MAZUR

Are you my mother's real daughter Rona asked me after Bertha died.

LYNDA STURNER

2

THE STORY'S HISTORY

In "First Sentences: Beginning in the Middle," we illustrate how most stories and novels begin in situation, in the middle of things. But, you might ask, what about the "beginning" of the story itself? Well, a few years ago, during the discussion of a flashback, a student said, "You mean it's as if every story has its own memory, its own history." Yes, that is exactly right. Each story has a history; all characters have pasts; the plots of most stories or novels are affected by something that happened before sentence one on the first page. Yet this history is woven so skillfully into the narrative of the story that most times we don't realize we are actually reading about the past of the story.

It might be helpful to think of the story as a straight line with sentence one appearing somewhere beyond the start of the line—ideally near the middle. At some point, most stories or novels dip back into the past, to the beginning of the straight line and catch the reader up on the situation—how and why X has gotten himself into such a pickle with character Y. Tolstoy's novel *Anna Karenina* starts off with a household in a flutter over the husband's affair with the governess. Margaret Atwood's novel *Life Before Man* starts *after* someone has committed suicide. Yet these events foreshadow and affect the stories to come. The forward movement of Flannery O'Connor's "A Good Man Is Hard to Find" is so compelling that it is easy to overlook how the grandmother's past informs the action of the story. And the past of Amy Hempel's story "Today Will Be a Quiet Day" is filled with ominous events: children's fights that led the father to say he wanted "Today will be a quiet day" written on his tombstone; the parents' divorce; the boy's friend who told the boy, "never play Ping-Pong with a mental patient because it's all we do and we'll kill you" and who later

7

committed suicide; the kids learning the guillotine joke; the dog that had to be put to sleep—all this before page one. That's good writing.

THE EXERCISE

First, return to a favorite story and make a list of events that occurred before page one. Ask: How do these events affect the story after page one and move the story to resolution? Do this exercise with several stories and novels.

Then look at a draft of one of your own stories. Take notes on your story's history. Does your story have a past? A history all its own? Is the current situation grounded in the history of the story? You might discover that your stories have a case of amnesia—a lack of history that makes the current situation thin or lacking in alternatives and tension.

THE OBJECTIVE

To understand how stories and novels—and the characters in those stories and novels—all have a history that affects their forward movement and resolution.

3

PAIRS OF BEGINNING SENTENCES

from Alexandra Marshall

Sometimes less is more, and sometimes it is just less. But no matter what, writing with a strict economy of purpose can force useful answers to fundamental questions. Even from one sentence you can learn both who the character is and what the story is about. To provide focus, it is helpful to begin by writing sentences in arbitrary pairs with established parameters.

THE EXERCISE

Write the first sentence of a story about a birth. Now write the first sentence about a death. Try other pairs, such as falling in love and filing for divorce. Try pairs that are not in opposition, such as spring and summer. Then invent your own pairs.

THE OBJECTIVE

This is a way to sharpen skill by working for a specific kind of clarity. It is about naming essences.

STUDENT EXAMPLE

A birth and a death
1. I won't be doing any bonding with either one of them for quite a while; I knew I shouldn't have gone into the delivery room.

2. "He doesn't look peaceful or tortured or saintly, and no, he doesn't look 'just like himself'; he looks like some dead thing that I never knew, and I don't know why I'm here."

Falling in love and filing for divorce
1. It could have happened to him a dozen times before and with women prettier, smarter, richer, funnier, sexier, even nicer, but it didn't, did it?

2. I don't want to throw her out the window or cheat her out of the money or tell her what a shit she is; I want to thank her for every goddamn day of it.

Spring and summer
1. All spring means to me is that things change, and if they didn't, I'd never die—but I'd want to.

2. The end of summer stopped having any tangible meaning in his life long ago, but with each year he is still slower to recover from it.

CHRISTOPHER LYNCH

4

BEGIN A STORY WITH
A "GIVEN" FIRST LINE

from William Kittredge

It can be challenging to begin a story with a "given" first line—especially one that starts in the middle. You can use a line from a poem, make one up, or use the one in this exercise. Or ask a friend or fellow writer to give you a first line—this is what Doris Lessing's characters do in her novel, *The Golden Notebook.* When we come to the place in the novel where Saul gives Anna the first line "The two women were alone in the London flat," we realize that Anna did write her book, and that *The Golden Notebook,* which begins with that exact line, is Anna's novel.

THE EXERCISE

Begin a story with this line: Where were you last night?

THE OBJECTIVE

The objective is to once more start the story *in medias res*—in the middle of things. Notice how this question begins in the middle of a situation. For example, "last night," the subject of the question, has already happened. If one character asks another this question there are already two people "on stage." And the question will probably produce a conflict. But don't get hung up on making it a line of dialogue—it can be used many different ways.

STUDENT EXAMPLES

Where were you last night was the one thing she couldn't ask him anymore, so they talked about the death of Huey Newton. They were in the kitchen having breakfast, Marcy was eating

11

Special K and Tom, Shredded Wheat. As usual, he had bought two copies of the *Times* and they each came upon the story at the same time. Twenty-three years had gone by since they had met and fallen in love during the height of the demonstrations at Berkeley and now Huey Newton was as dead as their marriage.

LYNDA STURNER

"Where were you last night?" Rob asked.

Eric kicked at the gravel. He knew he'd hear that question as soon as he saw Rob. They had planned to meet under the Grolsch sign by Flanagan's back alley. It was going to be a nice smooth operation. Ski masks, two unloaded guns. In and out before old Flanagan knew what hit him. They had everything planned, including which brand of gin—Gordon's—Rob would grab off the shelf before they ran out of the store. It would have worked perfectly, if Eric had showed up. That was precisely why he hadn't.

PAULA A. LaFONTAINE

Where was I last night and how did I get here? I am lying on the sofa in my old apartment where my ex-boyfriend, Roy, still lives. The afghan I made for him a year earlier is draped over me. I pull it up to my chin. It smells like Roy: Old Spice and Camel filters.

Maria walks out of my old bedroom wearing Roy's blue and white striped Oxford. "You're awake," she says. "Roy says I have to let you stay here as long as you want."

I sit up. My head hurts and my teeth taste like vodka. From Chessy's Bar and Grill. I ran into Roy over by the pinball machines. He made me give him my car keys. They are on the coffee table now, next to my bag and earrings.

"Have a little too much, Janis?" Maria walks past me to the kitchen.

I stand up, holding the arm of the sofa. "Where's Roy?"

Maria puts enough water on for one cup of coffee. "He opens the 7-Eleven on Saturdays. Don't you remember?"

CHRISTY VELADOTA

"Where you last night?" Tony asked, wiping down the bar in front of me with a gray towel. He doesn't look me in the eye.

"Vegas," I said, fingering an earring, noticing how bald he is, how short. "Where do you think?" Of course, I didn't really

12

spend the night in Vegas or in any place worth mentioning, but when you're forty-one and planted on a bar stool, it's nice to think you still have possibilities, even if you can only reach them in your head.

BRIDGET MAZUR

Anecdotes don't make good stories. Generally I dig down underneath them so far that the story that finally comes out is not what people thought their anecdotes were about.

ALICE MUNRO

5

WAYS TO BEGIN A STORY

from Robie Macauley

THERE ARE MANY DIFFERENT MEANS A WRITER MIGHT USE TO BEGIN a story, and the problem is to choose one that most appropriately raises the curtain on the narrative to follow. Ask yourself such questions as these: Do I want my story to open with the sound of voices as people discuss something about their lives? Or do I want to bring one important character forward into the descriptive spotlight and let the reader have a good, long look at her before action begins? Or do I want to begin with an activity—one person, or more than one, engaged in doing something that will be significant for the story to follow? To judge these three possible openings, the writer might then ask questions of the unwritten story: Story, are you going to be about some involvement of people and their attitudes and opinions; are the ways they voice their thoughts going to be important? Or, Story, are you going to concern yourself with the traits, ideas, experiences, and emotions of one person who must seize the reader's imagination at once? Or are you going to be involved with an event—or events—in which the characters take part, and thus you want an opening that shows actions? Here are some of the possible ways of leading off.

With a generalization

My mother believed you could be anything you wanted to be in America.

AMY TAN, "Two Kinds"

When people become characters, they cease to be regarded as human, they are something to be pointed out, like the orange tree that President Kruger planted, the statue in the park, or the filling station that once was the First Church hall.

NADINE GORDIMER, "The Last Kiss"

With a description of a person

He was lifting his knees high and putting his hand up, when I first saw him, as if crossing the road through that stringing rain, he were breaking through the bead curtain of a Pernambuco bar. I knew he was going to stop me.

V. S. PRITCHETT, "The Sailor"

With narrative summary

An unfortunate circumstance in my life has just recalled to mind a certain Dr. Crombie and the conversations I used to hold with him when I was young. He was the school doctor until the eccentricity of his ideas became generally known.

GRAHAM GREENE, "Doctor Crombie"

With dialogue

"Don't think about a cow," Matt Brinkley said.

ANN BEATTIE, "In the White Night"

I'm afraid Walter Cronkite has had it, says Mom.

JAYNE ANNE PHILLIPS, "Home"

With several characters but no dialogue

During the lunch hour, the male clerks usually went out, leaving myself and three girls behind. While they ate their sandwiches and drank their tea, they chattered away thirteen to the dozen. Half their conversation I didn't understand at all, and the other half bored me to tears.

FRANK O'CONNOR, "Music When Soft Voices Die"

15

With a setting and only one character

After dinner, with its eight courses and endless conversation, Olga Mikhailovna, whose husband's birthday was being celebrated, went out into the garden. The obligation to smile and talk continuously, the stupidity of the servants, the clatter of dishes, the long intervals between courses, and the corset she had put on to conceal her pregnancy from her guests, had wearied her to the point of exhaustion.

ANTON CHEKHOV, "The Birthday Party"

With a reminiscent narrator

I was already formally engaged, as we used to say, to the girl I was going to marry.

PETER TAYLOR, "The Old Forest"

With a child narrator

I don't have much work to do around the house like some girls.

TONI CADE BAMBARA, "Raymond's Run"

When I was in the third grade I knew a boy who had to have fourteen shots in the stomach as the result of a squirrel bite.

ELLEN GILCHRIST, "Victory over Japan"

By establishing point of view

First person
Since Dr. Wayland was late and there were no recent newsmagazines in the waiting room, I turned to the other patient and said: "As a concerned person, and as your brother, I ask you, without meaning to offend, how did you get that scar on the side of your face?"

JAMES ALAN McPHERSON, "The Story of a Scar"

There was no exchange of body fluids on the first date, and that suited both of us just fine.

T. CORAGHESSAN BOYLE, "Modern Love"

16

I'm Push the bully, and what I hate are new kids and sissies, dumb kids and smart, rich kids, poor kids, kids who wear glasses, talk funny, show off, patrol boys and wise guys and kids who pass pencils and water the plants—and cripples, especially cripples.

STANLEY ELKIN, "Criers and Kibitzers,
Kibitzers and Criers"

Third person
The August two-a-day practice sessions were sixty-seven days away, Coach calculated.

MARY ROBISON, "Coach"

Climbing up with a handful of star decals to paste on the bathroom ceiling, Claire sees a suspect-looking shampoo bottle on the cluttered top shelf.

FRANCINE PROSE, "Other Lives"

THE EXERCISE

This one is in two parts. First experiment with different types of openings for different stories until you feel comfortable with the technique of each. Then see how many ways there are to open one particular story you have in mind. How does the story change when the opening changes from a generalization to a line of dialogue?

THE OBJECTIVE

To see how experimenting with several ways of opening your story can lead you to a better understanding of whose story it is, and what the focus of the story will be.

II: NOTEBOOKS AND JOURNALS
AND MEMORY

I<small>N A CARTOON BY</small> W<small>ILLIAM</small> H<small>AMILTON, A HARASSED-LOOKING YOUNG</small> woman is seated at a desk, holding some manuscript pages. Her typewriter momentarily has been pushed to one side, as she says into the phone, "Frances, can I get back to you? Gordon ran away with the babysitter and I'm trying to see if there's a short story in it."

Of course there's a story in it. Probably several, but now might be a little soon to begin writing about Gordon's flight. Hamilton's young woman needs to take to heart what Wordsworth said about poetry, that it is "emotion recollected in tranquillity."

What this young woman should do, since she is determined to find a story, is jot down in a notebook or journal a few details that she doesn't want to lose. Perhaps Gordon left an odd note? Or one of the children asked if Gordon, who had recently lost his Wall Street job, was going to start a babysitting business. Or perhaps the harassed young wife discovered she was secretly delighted that Gordon was gone?

When she returns to this material at a later time, if she does, she might want to tell the story from Gordon's point of view—a story about a man who leaves his wife because he knows that she will someday leave him. Or from the babysitter's point of view—a story about a babysitter who feels sorry for a husband whose wife begins typing the minute he gets home from work.

The point is, as writers we lead double lives. We live in the world as the people we are—but we also live in the world as writer/observers ready to see a story anywhere, to note a detail that simply couldn't be made up, to record an overheard line of dialogue, to explore our enemies' points of view, and to sift through memory—did we really have a happy childhood? A writer's notebooks and journals are a testimony to this double life. As Socrates said, "The unexamined life is not worth living."

Journals and notebooks function in several ways. One writer may use them as a repository for the raw material for fiction that he will return to for inspiration. Another writer may keep a notebook but never look at what he writes again—for him, the act of selecting and writing something down was the valuable exercise, keeping his writer's ear and eye in shape. And yet another writer may use her journal for deepening stories she's already written.

Our exercises are designed to show you some of the possibilities and rewards of keeping a journal or notebook. It is the perfect place to jot down that odd name you found on a program—"Buck Gash"—a name you'll never legally be able to use, but one you want to remember. Or to make a list of all the places you've ever lived. Or to write a journal entry from the point of view of the babysitter titled "Why I'm running away tomorrow with Mr. Farnham (I call him 'Gordie')."

6

WHO ARE YOU?
SOMEBODY!

Richard Hugo, in an essay titled "In Defense of Creative Writing Classes," recalls the most important lesson he ever learned, "perhaps the most important lesson one can teach. You are someone and you have a right to your life." He decries the way the world tells us in so many ways that "individual differences do not exist" and that "our lives are unimportant." He says, "A creative writing class may be one of the last places you can go where your life still matters." The same thing is true for the writer who sits alone at her desk.

THE EXERCISE

Buy a notebook to use for just this one exercise. Then, on a regular basis, perhaps at the beginning of your writing time or before you go to bed, write for ten to twenty minutes addressing each of the following subjects:

- List in detail all the places you have lived—one place per page. (This is a good way to begin because it gives the entire notebook a concrete grounding in time and place.) You might even want to get very specific, say, by recounting all the kitchens, or bedrooms.
- Next, recall if you were happy or unhappy in those places.
- Consider your parents' relationship, from their point of view.
- List important family members: brothers and sisters, grandparents, uncles and aunts, cousins. What were the dynamics of your nuclear family, your extended family? (Some of these subjects may take several twenty-minute sessions. Leave space for unfinished business.)

21

■ List smells—indoor and outdoor—and the memories they conjure up.
■ Do you have any recurring dreams or nightmares? Start a section for dreams.
■ Ask yourself, What did I care about when I was five, ten, fifteen, twenty, twenty-five, thirty, etc.? What do I care about now?
■ What is your five-year plan?

These are the kinds of questions that help you define who you are. Now make up questions of your own to answer in your notebook. In fact, making up questions to bring back the past, to explore the present, and to voice your hopes and expectations for the future is part of the fun of this exercise.

OBJECTIVE

To lead an examined life. Your notebook will become a lifetime companion and an invaluable source of material.

7

PUT YOUR HEART ON THE PAGE

In a letter to a young Radcliffe student, F. Scott Fitzgerald wrote of the price she must pay for aspiring to be a professional writer:

> You've got to sell your heart, your strongest reactions, not the little minor things that only touch you lightly, the little experiences that you might tell at dinner. This is especially true when you begin to write, when you have not yet developed the tricks of interesting people on paper, when you have none of the technique which it takes time to learn. When, in short, you have only your emotions to sell.

Too many writers avoid their own strongest feelings because they are afraid of them, or because they are afraid of being sentimental. Yet these are the very things that will make beginning work ring true and affect us. Your stories have to matter to you the writer before they can matter to the reader; your story has to affect you, before it can affect us. William Kittredge says, "If you are not *risking* sentimentality, you are not close to your inner self."

THE EXERCISE

Make a notebook entry on an early childhood event that made you cry or terrified you, or that made you weak with shame or triumphant with revenge. Then write a story about that event. Take us back to those traumatic times, relive them for us through your story in such a way so as to make your experience ours.

THE OBJECTIVE

To learn to identify events in your life that are still capable of making you laugh and cry. If you can capture these emotions and put them on paper, chances are you will also make your readers laugh and cry as well.

I have lost too much by losing, or rather by not having acquired, the note-taking habit. It might be of great profit to me; and now that I am older, that I have more time, that the labour of writing is less onerous to me, and I can work more at my leisure, I ought to endeavor to keep, to a certain extent, a record of passing impressions, of all that comes, that goes, that I see, and feel, and observe. To catch and keep something of life—that's what I mean.

HENRY JAMES, *Notebooks*, November 25, 1881

8

PEOPLE FROM THE PAST; CHARACTERS OF THE FUTURE

Most of us have an unsettling memory of another child who loomed larger than life as we were growing up. Someone we resented, feared, hated, or envied. It might have been a sibling, a cousin, someone from the neighborhood, or someone from school. Often, that child—perhaps a little older or a little younger—had the power to make us take risks we would never have taken on our own, or had the power to make us miserable. This is the subject of Margaret Atwood's novel *Cat's Eye*, in which artist Elaine Risley is haunted by Cordelia, just such a childhood tormentor and "friend." Well, eventually these children grow up.

THE EXERCISE

First, think about your childhood between the ages of six and twelve and try to recall someone whose memory, even now, has the power to invoke strong, often negative feelings in you. Was that person the class bully, the clown, the daredevil, the town snob, the neighborhood bore, etc? Write down details of what you remember about this person. How she looked and talked. Did you ever have any encounters with this person. Or did you just observe her from a distance?

Next, if you haven't seen this person for ten years or longer imagine what she is doing now, where she lives, etc. Be specific.

If you had a long acquaintance with this person, or still know her, imagine where she will be ten years from now.

THE OBJECTIVE

To understand how our past is material for our imaginations and how writing well can be the best revenge.

STUDENT EXAMPLES

His first name was Frank, or Frankie. We went to a small private day school in California. There were thirteen students in my eighth grade class and all of us were afraid of Frankie who was in the ninth grade. He was the school bully, a mean person, bottom line.

Once when I walked into the locker room, Frankie threw a Japanese Ninja throwing star into the wall just next to me. "Damn, I missed," he said. He talked about how his father had hit him with a 2×4 and he'd asked him for more. He bragged that his father had shot and killed a black man. Frankie hated everyone.

I can imagine Frankie in ten years. He'll be a white supremacist living in rural Georgia and working in a factory. He'll be married with three kids. He'll keep loaded shotguns and pistols around the house and will threaten to kill the kids. Before he's 35 he'll be doing time for a murder he committed outside a bar.

HUNTER HELLER

Darlene was two years older than me, heavy set, a great football player. She loved the Dallas Cowboys just like all the guys—although we also liked the cheerleaders. Darlene taught me to ride a bike because she was sick of riding me around on her handlebars. One day, she put me on her Sears ten-speed and pushed me into the street, where I smashed into a parked car. She got mad because I "messed up the paint" on her bike. She says I ruined her first sexual experience one night when all the neighborhood kids were playing "Ring-O-Leveo." According to her, she was under a bush, about to "make her move" on Jeremy Witkins, when I saw her and called out her name and location. We used to smoke Marlboro Reds and drink stolen Budweisers behind the local swimming pool. In the five years I knew her, she never once wore a skirt.

I'll bet Darlene went to Grattenville Trade school—she was tough and good with tools. She probably kept wearing concert-Tee's, denim jackets, and eventually got into heavy metal. I wonder if her teeth got straightened and her acne went away and her breasts got even bigger. I can imagine her dropping out of school, fighting with her folks all the time, and scooping ice cream nine to five at Carvel, or selling 36-shot film out the little Fotomat window. She'll buy takeout most nights. I can see her standing in line for a couple of beers and a slice of pepperoni for her live-in boyfriend, a muffler mechanic named Al, who is too high to deal with the counter person.

DANIEL BIGMAN

I never travel without my diary. One should always have something sensational to read in the train.

OSCAR WILDE

27

9

MINING MEMORY

ALMOST INVARIABLY, THE BEGINNING WRITER VIEWS HIS LIFE AS DULL. The opposite is true—your own life is teeming with incident and emotion. Train yourself to identify and store away for future use the odd, funny, sad, and suspenseful things that happen to you.

THE EXERCISE

Over the period of a week or so write down ten things that made you angry, but don't try to explain why. Over the same time period do the same for ten things that pleased you. Be very specific. Statements like "I felt good when I woke up on Wednesday morning," are too vague to carry any conviction—and this could have happened to anyone. "I ran into Ms. Butler, my third-grade teacher, in the Star Market and she said hello to me by my right name" is specific and could only have happened to you.

THE OBJECTIVE

You may not use most of what you've written down, but you will have practiced viewing your immediate world as a garden full of fictional seeds.

STUDENT EXAMPLE

Things that pleased me
1. Plastic pumpkins and Indian corn at the supermarket checkout.
2. Little girls in winged Viking helmets on Leif Eriksson Day.

3. On Columbus Day, lying in my bed listening to fireworks—muffled explosions which come faster and faster as the show reaches its finale.
4. Jeff's example of slang peculiar to his household: "Week to be" means a person's week off from the chore wheel.
5. Carolyn's new job: painting wooden toys for children.
6. In a cleanly swept fireplace, a little stuffed mouse with red ears.
7. Glancing at my Harmony textbook as I'm getting dressed in the morning, and then suddenly remembering a dream from the night before.
8. A pet rabbit with floppy ears like a dachshund's.
9. After I order a peanut butter frappé with chocolate syrup, the woman in line behind me laughs and says she's going to order the same.
10. Jeff's roommate, on a postcard from France, lists the French grammar books he has bought there.

Things that made me angry
1. Heidi walking through the door and then, without saying hello, beginning to complain about the money in the household fund.
2. In the Catholic school playground, kids playing "Duck, duck, goose" while a nun stands watching them.
3. Eric's looking away coldly when Don shakes his hand.
4. Smelling Dunkin' Donuts from half a block away.
5. Learning that *Boston Magazine* readers have an average annual income of $110,000.
6. A smelly man in a dirty sweatshirt browsing near me in the Boston Public Library.
7. The padlocked wooden box where Jeff's neighbor keeps laundry detergent.
8. The bathroom door swinging loose as the pin in the top hinge snaps in half.
9. The teenager in line at Tower Records with a denim jacket covered with buttons from trendy pop bands—Love and Rockets, U2, Talking Heads, and many others.
10. My bedroom window cracking in half in the wind.

MIKE RASHIP

10

CHANGING YOUR LIFE

from Joy Nolan

Art is art because it is *not* nature. —Goethe

Good fiction has a confluence of detail that real life seldom has. We've all been told "write what you know," and its true that autobiographical material enriches fiction with vivid details. But don't sell your fiction short by sticking to the facts— what you know extends far past the specific incidents of your life. The more flexible and elastic your use of facts and feelings borrowed from life, the stronger your writing will be. Marcel Proust said, "Creative wrong memory is a source of art."

As a writer of fiction, you have to be more loyal to the fiction than to the facts that inspired it. Remembering being chased by a vicious dog as a child may give you just the right flavor of terror to vividly describe a thief's fear while fleeing the police in your story. Or you can invest a fictional event with remembered emotion, or use a real-life scene as a backdrop for your imagination, changing the feelings and consequences entirely.

THE EXERCISE

Choose a central dramatic incident from your life.

- Write about it in first person, and then write about it in third person (or try second person!). Write separate versions from the point of view of each character in the incident.
- Have it happen to someone ten or twenty years older or younger than yourself.

30

■ Stage it in another country or in a radically different setting.
■ Use the skeleton of the plot for a whole different set of emotional reactions.
■ Use the visceral emotions from the experience for a whole different story line.

THE OBJECTIVE

To become more fluent in translating emotions and facts from truth to fiction. To help you see the components of a dramatic situation as eminently elastic and capable of transformation. To allow your fiction to take on its own life, to determine what happens and why in an artful way that is organic to the story itself. As Virginia Woolf said, "There must be great freedom from reality."

11

JOURNAL KEEPING FOR WRITERS

from William Melvin Kelley

Everybody has a day to write about, and so writing about the day makes everybody equal. Diary keeping separates the act of writing from creating character and plot. You can write every day and learn certain fictional techniques without having to invent fiction on command.

THE EXERCISE

Write one page a day. Concentrate on observation and description, not feeling. For example, if you receive a letter, the ordinary reaction is to write in the diary, "I received a letter that made me happy." (Or sad.) Instead, describe the size of the envelope, the quality of the paper, what the stamps looked like.

Keep your diary without using the verb *to be*. Forms of the verb *to be* don't create any vivid images. By avoiding its use, you get into the habit of choosing more interesting verbs. You'll also be more accurate. For example, some people will say "John Smith is a really funny guy," when what they really mean is "John Smith makes me laugh." Or "I like John Smith's sense of humor."

Experiment with sentence length. Keep the diary for a week in sentences of ten words or less. Then try writing each day's account in a single sentence. Avoid use of "and" to connect the long sentence; try out other conjunctions.

Switch your diary to third person for a while, so that instead of writing *I*, you can write about *he* or *she*. Then, try mixing the point of view. Start the day in third person and switch into first person to comment on the action. By interspersing first- and third-person points of view, you can experiment with stream of consciousness and the interior monologue.

Try keeping your diary in an accent—first the accent of somebody who is learning how to write English, then the accent of somebody learning to speak English.

Keep it in baby talk: Baby want. Baby hurt. Baby want food. Baby want love. Baby walk.

Try making lists for a diary entry—just a record of the nouns of that day: toothbrush, coffee, subway tokens, schoolbooks, gym shoes.

THE OBJECTIVE

To enhance your powers of observation and description without having to juggle the demands of characterization and plot.

III: CHARACTERIZATION

Wʜᴇɴ ʏᴏᴜ ᴍᴇᴇᴛ sᴏᴍᴇᴏɴᴇ ғᴏʀ ᴛʜᴇ ғɪʀsᴛ ᴛɪᴍᴇ, ʏᴏᴜ ɪᴍᴍᴇᴅɪᴀᴛᴇʟʏ begin to make a judgment about her, an assessment partly conscious and partly instinctive. You take in, for instance, her clothes, her haircut, the type of watch—if any—she wears. When she talks you notice her accent and vocabulary and especially what she says to you. You see if she smiles easily or whether she seems standoffish. These are just a few of the clues you process intuitively.

As a writer, you owe it to your readers to supply your characters with just such a host of clues. The more specific you make these attributes, the more immediate your characters will be. Thus characterization means fleshing out the people who inhabit your fiction by providing them with physical characteristics, habits and mannerisms, speech patterns, attitudes, beliefs and motives, desires, a past and a present, and finally, actions. This last attribute—how your characters act in a given situation—will determine your character's future (as she is further revealed through action) and shape the forward movement and final resolution of your story. As Heracleitus said, "Character is destiny."

Now, where fully realized characters come from is another story. Perhaps it is best summed up by Graham Greene when he says, "One never knows enough about characters in real life to put them into novels. One gets started and then, suddenly, one can not remember what toothpaste they use; what are their views on interior decoration, and one is stuck utterly. No, major characters emerge; minor ones may be photographed." One place that characters can emerge from is your notebooks. For example, read F. Scott Fitzgerald's notebooks to see how a writer's mind works. He even had classifications for notes such as C—Conversation and Things Overheard, P—Proper Names; H—Descriptions of Humanity, etc. Notebooks are a good place to collect names, lines of dialogue, and those details you just couldn't make up—like the guy we saw on the subway who, just before he got off, carefully tucked his wet chewing gum into his ear.

12

HE/SHE: SWITCHING GENDER

As a writer of fiction you're seriously handicapped if you can't write convincingly about people unlike yourself. You should be able to assume the voice (or, at least, the point of view) of a child, an old person, a member of the opposite gender, or someone of another race. An accomplished writer assumes as many shapes, sizes, colors, etc. as the fictional occasions demand. This requires you to do what actors do when taking on a role: they not only imagine what it's like to be another person, they transform themselves, they get inside their character's skin. The following passage is from Anne Bernays's novel *Professor Romeo*, in which the author, using the third person, writes from a man's point of view:

> "Why do all you girls think you're fat? [Barker asks]" "Even you skinny ones?"
> "You really think I'm skinny?"
> Barker saw Kathy's teeth for the first time as she grinned at him. He had almost forgotten that bit of magic: tell a female she's thin and she's yours for life.

In *A Handful of Dust*, Evelyn Waugh's protagonist, Brenda Last, has all the inflections of a woman trying to convince her husband that she's not an adulteress (which she is.) Here, she tells her husband over the phone about the apartment she's taken. "Well, there are a good many smells at present and the bath makes odd sounds and when you turn on the hot tap there's a rush of air and that's all and the cold tap keeps dripping and the water is rather brown . . . and the curtains won't pull right across. . . . But it's *lovely.*"

THE EXERCISE

Write a page in the first person, assuming the voice of someone of the opposite gender. This can be a description, a narrative, or a segment of autobiography. The main point is to completely lose yourself and become another.

THE OBJECTIVE

To learn how to draw convincing verbal portraits of characters different from yourself and to make them sympathetic, rounded, and complex even though you don't especially "like" them or admire what they represent.

STUDENT EXAMPLE

Since I broke my hip I haven't been out of the apartment in three months. A young lady—she couldn't be more than sixteen or seventeen—brings in two meals a day, breakfast and supper. I either have to get my own lunch or go hungry. She comes in carrying a tray covered in silver foil. Her name is Debby and she works for the state.

It must have been a shock for Debby the first time she saw me naked. I wasn't expecting her that early and it was end of July and hot as blazes. I tried to cover my parts, but I wasn't quite quick enough. She looked away and said "I've brought you some waffles, Mr. Pirjo, I hope you like them." Then she made herself busy getting me my knife and fork, but I could see she was upset. Why didn't they tell me she was coming at eight in the morning?

Every time Debby comes by I ask her to stay a while and sit down and have a cup of coffee with me but she says she has five more people on her list or something like that; she's in and out of here so fast, she's like a little rabbit who you only see the tail of.

JUDITH HOPE

Fiction is nothing less than the subtlest instrument for self-examination and self-display that mankind has invented yet.

JOHN UPDIKE

13

FUNNY—YOU DON'T LOOK SEVENTY-FIVE

Rᴇᴀᴅᴇʀs ɴᴇᴇᴅ ᴛᴏ ᴋɴᴏᴡ ᴄᴇʀᴛᴀɪɴ ʙᴀsɪᴄ ꜰᴀᴄᴛs ᴀʙᴏᴜᴛ ʏᴏᴜʀ ᴄʜᴀʀ-acters. They should have some idea of their appearance and approximately how old they are. A writer can, of course, say something direct, like "Marvin Highsmith, sixty-eight years old, owned a Chevy pickup." But it's more interesting and dramatic to *suggest* a character's age, rather than to present the reader with a naked number. In the following passage from *Memento Mori* by Muriel Spark, an aged woman makes herself a pot of tea; the entire enterprise is made to seem Herculean—as indeed it is for a very old person. Spark never steps in to "tell" the reader that Charmian is in her eighties; it's all done through Charmian's perceptions.

Charmian made her way to the library and cautiously built up the fire which had burnt low. The effort of stooping tired her and she sat for a moment in the big chair. After a while it was tea-time. She thought, for a space, about tea. Then she made her way to the kitchen where the tray had been set by Mrs. Anthony in readiness for Mrs. Pettigrew to make the tea. But Mrs. Pettigrew had gone out. Charmian felt overwhelmed suddenly with trepidation and pleasure. Could she make tea herself? Yes, she would try. The kettle was heavy as she held it under the tap. It was heavier still when it was half-filled with water. It rocked in her hand and her skinny, large-freckled wrist ached and wobbled with the strain. At last she had lifted the kettle safely on to the gas ring. She had seen Mrs. Anthony use the automatic lighter. She tried it but could not make it work. Matches. . . . At last the gas was lit under the kettle. Charmian put the teapot on the stove to warm. She then sat down in Mrs. Anthony's chair to wait for the kettle to boil. She felt strong and fearless.

When the kettle had boiled she spooned tea into the pot

and knew that the difficult part had come. She lifted the kettle a little and tilted its spout over the tea-pot. She stood as far back as she could. In went the hot water, and though it splashed quite a bit on the stove, she did not get any over her dress or her feet. She bore the tea-pot to the tray. It wafted to and fro, but she managed to place it down gently after all.

She looked at the hot-water jug. Should she bother with hot water? She had done so well up to now, it would be a pity to make any mistake and have an accident. But she felt strong and fearless. A pot of tea without the hot-water jug beside it was nonsense. She filled the jug, this time splashing her foot a little, but not enough to burn.

When all was set on the tray she was tempted to have her tea in the kitchen there in Mrs. Anthony's chair.

But she thought of her bright fire in the library. She looked at the tray. Plainly she could never carry it. She would take in the tea-things one by one, even if it took half-an-hour.

... First the tea-pot, which she placed on the library hearth. Then the hot-water jug. These were the dangerous objects. Cup and saucer; another cup and saucer in case Godfrey or Mrs. Pettigrew should return and want tea; the buttered scones; jam; two plates, two knives, and two spoons. Another journey for the plate of Garibaldi biscuits which Charmian loved to dip in her tea.... Three of the Garibaldi biscuits slid off the plate and broke on the floor in the hall. She proceeded with the plate, laid it on a table, and then returned to pick up the broken biscuits, even the crumbs.... Last of all she went to fetch the tray itself, with its pretty cloth. She stopped to mop up the water she had spilt by the stove. When she had brought everything into the room she closed the door, placed the tray on a low table by her chair and arranged her tea-things neatly upon it. The performance had taken twenty minutes.

When you start thinking about it you'll realize how many instant calculations you make when you first meet someone, assessing hair, eyes, girth, jawline and wrinkles. There are literally scores of clues on the human body. There are also indirect clues, like what sort of clothes the person is wearing, her verbal style and idiom; even the way she meets your eyes.

THE EXERCISE

Make a list of some of the ways you can suggest approximate age. Wrinkles and gray hair are the most obvious. Many are more subtle. You should be able to list at least a dozen.

THE OBJECTIVE

To make the best use of your powers of observation. The more precise the detail, the more convincing it is. How a person adjusts to the aging process tells us a good deal about her personality—this is as true for a fictional character as for a real one.

STUDENT EXAMPLE

Condition of teeth; presence of obvious dentures.
In a man—how much hair
Condition of hearing
What the T-shirt says
What sort of shoes she is wearing
Condition of skin
Posture
Quality and timbre of voice; idiom
Walking pace
Where found on Saturday night

STANLEY MONROE

14

NAMING YOUR CHARACTERS

WHEN YOU NAME A BABY YOU'RE TAKING A REAL CHANCE, BECAUSE you have no idea how the little tyke is going to turn out; we all know people whose names seem to belong to someone else. When you name a fictional character you have no excuse for getting it wrong because you should know him better than the members of your own family. The names you choose to give your characters should suggest certain traits, social and ethnic background, geography, and even things that have yet to occur in your story. Think of Vladimir Nabokov's Humbert Humbert and Henry James's Merton Densher—they just *sound* right. Charles Dickens was so adept at this subliminal skill that some of his characters' names have become generic, representing personality types—like Uriah Heep and, most notably, Ebenezer Scrooge. The names you choose have a strong and subtle influence on how your readers will respond to your characters. You may have to rename a character several times before you get it right.

THE EXERCISE

Name the following characters, keeping in mind that you can plant, within a name, a clue to their role in your fiction.

- A petty, white-collar thief who robs his boss over several years.
- An envious, bitter woman who makes her sister miserable by systematically trying to undercut her pleasure and self-confidence.
- A sweet young man too shy to speak to an attractive woman he sees every day at work.

■ The owner of a fast-food restaurant who comes on to his young female employees.
■ A grandmother who just won the lottery.

THE OBJECTIVE

To recognize that the names you give your characters should not be drawn out of a hat but carefully tested to see if they "work." Sometimes you may want to choose an "appropriate" name (Victoria for a member of the British aristocracy) and once in a while it's a good idea to choose a name that seems "inappropriate" (Bruce for the child of migrant farm workers). In each case, you are sending a message to the reader about who the character is, where he came from and where he is headed. A name can send a message as powerful as a title.

STUDENT EXAMPLE

Petty thief: Robin Blackman
Bitter woman: Mona Livitts
Shy young man: Tod Humbolt
Lecherous boss: Lenny Salsa
Lottery winner: Nana Shimpkis

JOAN CURLEY

15

OH! . . . THAT SORT OF PERSON

CAREFULLY CHOSEN DETAILS CAN REVEAL CHARACTER IN FASCINATING and different ways. Sometimes details tell something about the character described and also something different about the character making the observation. This is true of Anna Karenina's reaction on seeing her husband, Alexey Alexandrovitch, after a trip to Moscow, during which she patched up her brother's marriage and also met her future lover, Vronsky. Anna returns to St. Petersburg and is met at the train station by Alexey: " 'Oh, mercy! Why do his ears look like that?' she thought, looking at his frigid and imposing figure, and especially the ear that struck her at that moment as propping up the brim of his round hat." We see him as stern and ludicrous and we also feel her dismay as she becomes aware of her feelings toward him for the first time.

In other cases a character reveals more about himself than he suspects. For example, there is a vivid character in *The Great Gatsby* called Meyer Wolfsheim who calls Nick Carraway's attention to his cuff buttons and then boasts, "Finest specimens of human molars." Clearly, Wolfsheim means to impress his listener, but instead of charming Nick (or the reader), this detail has the opposite effect.

In *Rabbit, Run*, John Updike uses physical characteristics to account for Rabbit's nickname. "Rabbit Angstrom, coming up the alley in a business suit, stops and watches, though he's twenty-six and six three. So tall, he seems an unlikely rabbit, but the breadth of white face, the pallor of his blue irises, and a nervous flutter under his brief nose as he stabs a cigarette into his mouth partially explain the nickname, which was given to him when he too was a boy." And clearly, Rabbit is still appropriately called Rabbit, even though he's dressed in a suit and is no longer a boy.

The first lines of Bobbie Ann Mason's "Shiloh" also bring a character immediately to life. "Leroy Moffitt's wife, Norma Jean, is working on her pectorals. She lifts three-pound dumbbells to warm up, then progresses to a twenty-pound barbell. Standing with her legs apart, she reminds Leroy of Wonder Woman." By the end of the story, Norma Jean is working just as hard at improving her mind—and at not being Leroy's wife.

THE EXERCISE

First work with a story that you've already written, one whose characters need fleshing out. Write the character's name at the top of the page. Then fill in this sentence five or ten times:

He (or she) is the sort of person who _____ .

For example: Meyer Wolfsheim is the sort of person who boasts of wearing human molars for cuff links.

Then determine which details add flesh and blood and heart to your characters. After you have selected the "telling" detail, work it into your story more felicitously than merely saying, "She is the sort of person who . . ." Put it in dialogue, or weave it into narrative summary. But use it.

THE OBJECTIVE

To learn to select revealing concrete details, details that often tell us more than the character would want us to know.

16

WHAT DO YOU KNOW
ABOUT YOUR CHARACTERS?

I could take a battery of MMPI and Wonderlic personality
tests for each of my people and answer hundreds of questions
with as much intimate knowledge as if *they* were taking the
test.

—RICHARD PRICE

IN *DEATH IN THE AFTERNOON,* HEMINGWAY SAID, "PEOPLE IN A
novel, not skillfully constructed characters, must be projected
from the writer's assimilated experience, from his knowledge,
from his head, from his heart and from all there is of him. . . .
A good writer should know as near everything as possible."
Yet students frequently write stories about a major event in a
character's life, although they don't know some of the most
elementary things about that character—information that, if
known, most certainly would affect the character's motives and
actions.

Hemingway again speaks to this issue of being familiar with
characters.

If a writer of prose knows enough about what he is writing
about he may omit things that he knows and the reader, if the
writer is writing truly enough, will have a feeling of those
things as strongly as though the writer had stated them. The
dignity of movement of an iceberg is due to only one-eighth
of it being above water. A writer who omits things because
he does not know them only makes hollow places in his
writing.

THE EXERCISE

Work with one of your completed stories that has a character who needs fleshing out. Take out a sheet of paper and number from one to thirty-four. At the top of the page, write in the title of your story and the main character's name—and start filling in the blanks.

1. Character's name:
2. Character's nickname:
3. Sex:
4. Age:
5. Looks:
6. Education:
7. Vocation/occupation:
8. Status and money:
9. Marital status:
10. Family, ethnicity:
11. Diction, accent, etc.:
12. Relationships:
13. Places (home, office, car, etc.):
14. Possessions:
15. Recreation, hobbies:
16. Obsessions:
17. Beliefs:
18. Politics:
19. Sexual history:
20. Ambitions:
21. Religion:
22. Superstitions:
23. Fears:
24. Attitudes:
25. Character flaws:
26. Character strengths:
27. Pets:
28. Taste in books, music, etc.:
29. Journal entries:
30. Correspondence:
31. Food preferences:

32. Handwriting:
33. Astrological sign:
34. Talents:

No doubt you will be able to add to this list.

Note: This exercise should be done *after* you have written your story. It is not a way to conceive a character, but rather a way to reconceive a character. It is designed to discover what you know about your characters *after* you have written your story—and what you don't know. For example, one writer, Samuel R. Delany, tells his students to know exactly how much money their characters make and how they make it. And why not apply this list to some of your favorite stories? Note how much is known about the unforgettable grandmother in Flannery O'Connor's story "A Good Man Is Hard to Find" or about the compelling narrator in Peter Taylor's story "The Old Forest."

THE OBJECTIVE

To understand how much there is to know about a character that you have created. Of course, it is possible to write a successful story about a character without knowing everything on this list—or perhaps only knowing two or three things. On the other hand, beginning writers often don't know more than a character's age or gender—and frequently neglect an essential piece of information that would have greatly informed or shaped their story. You needn't include these details in the story, but their presence in your mind will be "felt" by the reader.

17

WHAT DO YOUR CHARACTERS WANT?

In her superb book *Writing Fiction*, Janet Burroway stresses the importance of knowing what characters *want:*

> It is true that in fiction, in order to engage our attention and sympathy, the central character must want and want intensely. The thing that character wants need not be violent or spectacular; it is the intensity of the wanting that counts. She may want only to survive, but if so she must want enormously to survive, and there must be distinct cause to doubt she will succeed.

Sometimes *want* is expressed in terms of *need, wish, hope,* etc.—and it is amazing how many times these words appear in the first two pages of stories.

Study the following examples to learn how *want* can drive a story.

> Mrs. Whipple loved her second son, the simple-minded one, better than she loved the other two children put together. . . .
> [She] hated to talk about it, she tried to keep her mind off it, but every time anybody set foot in the house, the subject always came up and she had to talk about Him first, before she could get on to anything else. It seemed to ease her mind. "I wouldn't have anything happen to him for all the world, but it just looks like I can't keep Him out of mischief. He's so strong and active, He's always into everything; He was like that since He could walk. . . . The preacher said such a nice thing once when he was here, and I'll remember it to my dying day, "The innocent walk with God—that's why He don't get hurt." Whenever Mrs. Whipple repeated those words, she always felt a warm pool spread in her breast, and the tears would fill her eyes, and then she could talk about something else.
> KATHERINE ANN PORTER, "He"

In the Gabriel García Márquez story "No One Writes to the Colonel," a colonel has been waiting for a certain letter for almost sixty years. As a young man, he had taken part in a successful revolution and, afterward, the government had promised him and other officers travel reimbursement and indemnities. The colonel's whole life has been a matter of marching in place and waiting ever since. Even though he has hired a lawyer, filed papers, written endlessly, and seen laws passed, nothing has happened. The lawyer notes that no official has ever taken responsibility. "In the last fifteen years, there have been seven Presidents, and each President changed his Cabinet at least ten times, and each Minister changed his staff at least a hundred times." The colonel says, "All my comrades died waiting for the mail"—but he refuses to give up, even though his life has been wasted and he has grown older, sicker, and crankier in the course of time.

The *want* that gives dynamic force to the story can take the form of a strong emotion, such as Mrs. Whipple's protective love; or an obsession, such as the colonel's determination to have his place in history recognized (probably his real motive); or it can be expressed in some specific plan or scheme.

Henry James's novel *The Wings of the Dove* is a good example of an elaborate scheme. Kate Croy, a London woman, knows that her one-time acquaintance Milly Theale, a rich and charming American, is dying of a mysterious disease. The doctors think that Milly's only chance for recovery lies in finding happiness—such as that of falling in love. Kate's scheme is to have her lover, Merton Densher, woo and marry Milly, inherit her money when she dies, and then marry Kate.

In Fitzgerald's *The Great Gatsby*, Jay Gatsby's whole ambition is to recover the past—specifically the idyllic time of his love affair with Daisy Buchanan years before.

Sometimes an ostensible *want* hides or overlays a greater one. Robert Jordan in Hemingway's *For Whom the Bell Tolls* intends to blow up a bridge to halt the advance of Franco's Fascist troops. But as he waits for the strategic moment, an underlying desire to experience the life of Spain and identify with the Spanish people emerges as his real *want*.

Leslie Epstein's *The King of the Jews* offers the reader an enigmatic mixture of purposes. I. C. Trumpelman, the Jewish puppet-leader whom the Nazis install as head of the ghetto wishes to preserve his people from the Holocaust—but he also has a drive to rule, dictate to, and punish them.

Wants in fiction aren't always simple and straightforward things, just as peoples' motives are seldom unmixed. The more complicated and unsuspected—both to her and to us—are a protagonist's aims, the more interesting that character will be and the more interesting will be the unfolding of her story.

THE EXERCISE

Look at the stories you've already written and ask

- What does the central character want?
- What are her motives for wanting this?
- Where in the story is this made clear to the reader?
- How do we learn what the central character wants? Dialogue? Actions? Interior thinking?
- What or who stands in the way of her achieving it?
- What does that desire set in motion?

If you don't know the answers to these questions, perhaps you don't know your character and her desires as well as you should. Aristotle said, "Man is his desire." What your central characters desire will inform the situations and ultimately the elements of the plots in which they are involved.

THE OBJECTIVE

To understand how your central character's desires shape her life. To see characterization as more than description and voice and mannerisms.

18

CREATING A CHARACTER'S BACKGROUND, PLACE, SETTING, AND MILIEU

from Robie Macauley

YOU ARE WHAT YOU BUY, OWN, EAT, WEAR, COLLECT, READ, AND CREate; and you are what you do for a living and how you live. If somebody broke into your home or apartment while you were away, chances are he could construct a good profile of who you are. You should be able to do exactly that for your characters even when they are "offstage."

THE EXERCISE

Create a setting for one or more of the following and furnish a place with his character—you create the character through observation of the setting. The place can be any kind of locale—house, a specific room in a house, outdoor grounds, an office, a cell, even a bed. The description must incorporate enough characteristic things so that the reader can visualize the absentee dweller accurately. Try to avoid stereotypes.

An unsuccessful painter
A former movie star who
    still thinks she's famous
A high-school senior about
    to flunk out
A cocktail waitress down
    on her luck
A blind person
A paraplegic

A member of a lunatic-
    fringe political group
A foster child
A fugitive from the law
A social climber
A paranoid person
A supermarket checkout
    woman who just won
    the state lottery

THE OBJECTIVE

To be able to select details that will create a character and furnish the world of that character. Note which details indicate the circumstances of the subject—such things as success or unsuccess, social status and habits. Which details indicate emotions, personality, intelligence, character, and outlook on life?

STUDENT EXAMPLE

Jeremy told me that after the accident his mother set up his room like the face of a clock. As I stand in the doorway, at what must be six o'clock, I see what he means.

Straight ahead, against the far wall is Jeremy's bed—twelve o'clock. His mom made the bed with tight hospital corners and his pajamas, black and white striped like a prisoner's uniform, are laid out for him.

His desk is at three o'clock. Braille copies of *A Tale of Two Cities* and *Wuthering Heights* sit next to a small cassette recordings of our Psych textbook. Tapes for American History, Econ., and Chemistry are stacked alongside.

I move to five o'clock and touch his empty bookcase. On the third shelf up, his initials, J.M.—Jeremy Malone—are etched deep in the wood. I close my eyes and run my fingers over them. Jeremy made this bookcase a year ago—about two months before his motorcycle accident on Route 9. Jeremy told his parents to take his books away.

The closet door, at nine o'clock, has been scrubbed with Murphy's Oil Soap. His stereo sits at ten o'clock, power off, but the volume turned nearly to its maximum. His posters of *Easy Rider* and the Budweiser girl are gone.

CHRISTY VELADOTA

19

DENY EVERYTHING

If you think the force of gravity is powerful, try breaking through the defenses of someone committed to denying the obvious. For example, tell the woman who falls for brutish men over and over again that she appears to court cruelty. Tell the man whose son is clearly a screwup, who keeps failing in school and hanging out with the worst crowd, that his son may need help, and the denying father will tell you that his kid is "going through a phase" or "sowing his wild oats." Denial is nearly impregnable; on the other hand, it can be useful in keeping someone from going over the edge.

THE EXERCISE

Write a two-person scene in which one character tries to break through another character's barrier of denial. Make the issue both specific and dramatic. Do this mainly in dialogue but anchor it in a particular time and place.

THE OBJECTIVE

To train yourself to be aware of the unconscious forces in everyday life. People are rarely what they seem; motives are cloudy at best and often almost entirely hidden. Fictional characters, like real ones, ought to incorporate this psychic complexity. Remember that occasionally *no* does mean *yes* and vice versa.

STUDENT EXAMPLE

The dinner dishes were washed, the dog walked, and Scott, Douglas and Patty Millbrook's fifteen-year-old son, had gone upstairs to watch television.

"Have you done your homework yet?" Douglas yelled after his son. "Remember, no television before homework."

"I've done it, Dad. I did it this afternoon."

"Good boy," Douglas said, and then turned to his wife, who was pouring two cups of coffee. "I have to say, I'm really pleased with how Scott's doing in school. I guess my pestering him all these years has really paid off. I mean, did you see his report card? Three A's and a B + ? A lot better than I ever did in school."

"Douglas, we have to talk. I got a call from Mr. Brand this afternoon."

"Who's Mr. Brand?" Douglas asked.

"Scott's English teacher," Patty said.

"Guess he wanted to tell us how great Scott's doing, right?"

"Not exactly," Patty said, sitting down at the table. "Sit down for a minute. Mr. Brand called because he thinks Scott has been cheating." Patty stared at her hands.

"What?" Douglas said, slamming down his coffee. "What did he say?"

"He thinks Scott's grades have gone up so suddenly because he's been cheating. He can't account for it any other way. Of course, I asked Scott, who denied it."

"You asked Scott? You mean you actually believe this Brand guy?" Douglas said. "No son of mine would ever cheat. This is the most absurd thing I've ever heard."

"I don't want to believe it either, but Scott's grades do seem to have jumped suddenly. Last semester he had a C in French and now he has an A. How do you explain that?"

"The boy's smart, Patty. He's finally learned the value of working hard. He's finally listened to me."

"But Douglas," Patty said, laying a hand on her husband's arm, "if anything, Scott's been studying less. Mr. Brand wanted to know if he was under a lot of pressure at home."

"What pressure? The kid's a normal, happy teenager."

"Maybe Scott feels so much pressure to do well that he has to resort to cheating. To please you."

"Great. Now this Brand guy is accusing me. Look, my old man put a lot of pressure on me and I turned out okay, didn't I? I didn't cheat."

"No, but you dropped out of high school, Doug. No one's saying this is your fault, but you *do* put a lot of pressure on Scott."

"You've been brainwashed, Patty. The kid's finally getting it right, and you all think he's cheating. I don't even want to discuss this anymore, and if that Mr. Brand has anything more to say, I'll set him straight. My son doesn't cheat, Patty. He's too smart for that."

HESTER KAPLAN

Look at Molly Bloom's soliloquy. To me, that's the ultimate proof of the ability of either sex to understand and convey the inner workings of the other. No woman was ever "written" better by a woman writer. How did Joyce know? God knows how and it doesn't matter.

NADINE GORDIMER, *Paris Review* interview

56

20

PSYCHIC CLOTHING

MOST OF US COVER THE NAKEDNESS OF OUR TRUE INTENTIONS WITH layers of psychic clothing. Our smile disguises a grimace; our laugh chokes a sob. The so-called text is right out there; the subtext is what is really going on. The two things don't necessarily have to contradict each other—they may vary only slightly. But it's important for the writer to be aware that subtexts exist, operating on a deeper, hidden level, along with overt action and dialogue.

In John Updike's story, "Still of Some Use," Foster and his former wife are cleaning out the attic of a house they once lived in together and which she is now selling.

" 'How can you bear it?' [Foster] asked of the emptiness.

"Oh, it's fun,' she said, 'once you get into it. Off with the old, on with the new. The new people seem nice. They have *little* children.' "

Nothing but pain lies beneath the wife's flippancy.

THE EXERCISE

Write two very short examples of text, in which the true meaning of the action or dialogue is hidden in a subtext. Under each text explicate the subtext.

THE OBJECTIVE

To learn to use indirection to illustrate the power of hidden meaning. This is something like a double exposure, a photograph that shows two images simultaneously.

STUDENT EXAMPLE

1. My dad is on the telephone. Instead of just talking about work and the weather, as usual, he says, "As you get older, you start to wonder about things—why we're here, or why there's anything at all."

Subtext: My mom is away in another state visiting my grandmother this week and my dad misses her.

2. When Ellen yells at a truck driver for driving past a parked school bus with its Stop sign out, Mrs. Roche, her next-door neighbor, leans out and says, "You should mind your own business." When Ellen explains that what the driver did was illegal and dangerous, Mrs. Roche says, "You just don't understand the situation. You ought to mind your own business."

Subtext: Mrs. Roche resents having a group of young people living on her block, which she feels belongs only to Irish Catholic families.

MIKE RASHIP

IV: PERSPECTIVE AND POINT OF VIEW

BEGINNING WRITERS SEEM BAFFLED BY THE TERM *POINT OF VIEW* (hereafter referred to as POV) and are constantly asking for an explanation of what it means—as if they didn't employ it every moment of their waking lives and even in their dreams.

We don't know why POV should furrow so many brows and cause such confusion. The term means precisely what it says, namely a particular angle of vision—which the writer then translates into words. For example, if you want to write about an automobile accident from the POV of the car's driver you would write it one way. If you chose the POV of the rescue crew who extracted the driver from the car, you would write it a different way. Two, three, four, people—and more—will each see the same event or person in a way slightly different from all the others.

The fiction writer can choose among several POVs with which to tell her story. The *omniscient* POV is not as popular today as it was in the nineteenth century. In telling a story from the omniscient POV, the author gets inside the heads of several characters and lets us know what each is thinking, moving around from one to another in turn so that the narrative has a many-faceted feel to it.

More usual in contemporary fiction is a POV restricted to one or two main, third-person—*he, she*—characters. We can learn about a failing marriage from the POV of the husband who suspects his wife of carrying on with their dentist. Or the author may feel that the story would be richer and denser to tell the story from the wife's POV as well. Obviously, each one of this unhappy pair will see things in a different light, with varied shading and color.

You may do a narrative from the first-person POV—the *I*. This *I* has a long and honorable tradition—"Call me Ishmael" is probably the most famous opening line in all of Western fiction. Then there is Nick Carraway's *I* in *The Great Gatsby*. In both these cases, the narrator is not the main character and, in one sense, is a stand-in for the author himself. A first-person narrative has the advantage of immediacy and a clear, singular voice—think of Holden Caulfield in *The Catcher in the Rye*. But if you write a story or novel using the first person POV, it's important to remember that the *I* should be present when most of the action takes place. She is almost continuously on stage or else in the wings, observing. (Anne Bernays wrote her novel *Growing Up Rich* using the third-person POV, then realized it belonged in the first person and rewrote the whole thing, starting on page one; it took a year. Changing POV like this involves a great deal more than simply turning all the *she*'s into *I*'s; the author must step out from the middle and let the *I*'s voice speak for itself.)

POV can also refer to a the particular time and distance the author chooses to tell her story from. For example, the exercise "An Early Memory, Part One" (p. 64) is from the POV of the narrator as a child; "An Early Memory, Part Two" (p. 67) is the same event written from the POV of the narrator as an adult. Naturally the sensibility, perspective, angle of vision, and moral stance will differ considerably in these two narratives.

POV should be no more daunting a concept than characterization. If you think of it as getting a fix on who in your story sees, hears, and feels what and how she processes the information, then you will avoid the common error of shifting unexpectedly from one character's POV to another.

21

THE ENGAGEMENT PARTY

Whenever you write in the first person you are, in a very real sense, getting inside the skin and psyche of the character through whose eyes you choose to unroll your narrative. It's important to know almost everything about this character whose mind and body you have chosen, for the duration of the story or novel, to inhabit. This can be extremely exhilarating, as it requires you to fantasize doing, saying, and experiencing things you may never do, for one reason or another, in real life. On the other hand, the first person has distinct limitations, the main one being that the author has to stay out of the picture and may not comment explicitly. The following exercise asks you to explore the possibilities inherent in the two POVs—first person and third.

THE EXERCISE

Write two separate versions of the same event: an engagement party. First write it with an *I* narrating, say the mother of the groom-to-be, and then use the third person. Notice how the fictional shadows fall differently in each version.

THE OBJECTIVE

To learn to feel easy in both the first and third person and to understand what the use of each entails, its potential and its problems.

STUDENT EXAMPLE

Part one
When I first met Jenny I thought she was a pretty little thing even though she has one of those really frizzy perms that the

girls down near Central Square seem to favor. I don't know *why* they do that to themselves. You should have seen her this afternoon, at the engagement party Bill and I gave for Tom. She was wearing this orange silk dress that was so tight you could see her panty line and her shoes had those sparkly things on the heels. Her mother and father were—oh dear, how shall I put this?—all over Bill. Her father came right out and asked Bill about the Money Club, you know, is it easy to get into and so on? I knew Bill was uncomfortable, because he wouldn't look Mr. O'Neill in the eye but he was very polite and muttered something about a waiting list. During all those toasts—Bill, Jenny's father, her sister Patty and that dreadful poem she insisted on reading—Jenny hung onto Tom as if he would flee if she took so much as her eyes off him. Maybe I shouldn't have done this at the party, but as soon as I could get Tom alone I told him that I hoped he could persuade Jenny to give up her job at the Canine Castle and go back to school. I can't understand why he gave me that frozen look of his. Can you imagine my mother knowing that a member of our family works as a dog groomer? I shouldn't say this, but it's probably just as well Mom's passed on.

Part two
Cynthia Hughes sighed and turned away from the middle of the Money Club's sun-bright main function room so she wouldn't have to look at Jenny O'Neill, the person her son Tom had—for a reason known only to God and maybe not even to him—to marry. The girl's dress was the limit, tight, tacky, and orange as the setting sun. Cynthia, a woman brought up in a time when you did certain things only because you were expected to and thus were spared long nights given over to making choices, was going through the motions of this engagement party like a trouper. And so, she saw and heard, was her husband, Bill. Just as the combo they'd hired to play golden oldies began to do "Michelle," Bill was accosted by Jenny's parents, Gloria and Jimmie O'Neill. Cynthia was disgusted—they had the gall to ask her long-suffering husband questions that sounded to her as if they were fishing for an invitation to join the Money Club, although they must— they should—have known that this was altogether out of the question. Cynthia walked away from this group; she didn't feel like mixing it up with the O'Neills. She helped herself to

62

a third glass of champagne from a waiter carrying a tray of them, and went to look for her son, whom she found by a large bay window that gave out over an immaculate slope of lawn; Jenny had both arms wrapped around Tom's right arm and was rubbing her tummy against his flank. Cynthia swerved so they wouldn't catch her looking at them. Later, when Tom had come temporarily unstuck from the adhesive Jenny, Cynthia had a chat with him.

It was a chat she regretted for months, for he lost his temper when she suggested that Jenny had "too much to offer— don't you think you could persuade her to quit her job at that dog place and go back to college?"

"Jenny loves her job, Mom," Tom said. "She loves animals and she's good at it. We don't have that kind of relationship. Maybe you try to persuade Dad to do things he doesn't want to but we don't believe in doing things that way. Back off, Mom."

Cynthia said, "If that's the way you're going to talk to me I'm sorry I said anything."

"Are you tipsy again, Mom?"

Cynthia shrugged and turned as Jenny came back from wherever it was she had been, probably the ladies room, trying to run a comb through the tangle of her frizzy permanent. For the first time, Cynthia was glad her own mother had not lived to see the day her favorite grandson would become engaged to a little fortune-hunting piece of goods like Jenny O'Neill.

AMY HOPE

22

AN EARLY MEMORY, PART ONE: THE CHILD AS NARRATOR

WRITE WHAT YOU KNOW" IS BY NOW SUCH A CLICHÉ THAT PEOPLE tend to ignore it. For the beginning writer it's pretty good advice. Your own life—and your memories of it—have an intensity and immediacy that are useful in creating fiction. It's not just what you know, however, but how you see it, shape it, and enhance it with your imagination. This is the crucial difference between fiction and fact. Fiction is always sifted through a singular set of perceptions, feelings, and wishes, while fact can be recorded by a machine designed for that purpose—a tape recorder or camera. Furthermore, the fiction writer often supplies an implicit rather than an explicit moral attitude.

THE EXERCISE

Using the present tense, write an early memory in the first person. This should be something that happened before you were seven. Use only those words and perceptions appropriate to a young child. "My father looks confused" won't do because a five-year-old is incapable of this articulation. "My father has a funny look on his face" is fine. The memory should be encapsulated in a short period of time—no more than an hour or so—and should happen in one place. Don't interpret or analyze; simply report it as you would a dream. When you can't remember details, make them up; you may heighten the narrative so long as you remain faithful to the "meaning" of the memory—the reason you recalled it in the first place. Limit: 550 words.

THE OBJECTIVE

A fiction writer should be able to present a narrative without nudging the reader or in any way explaining what she has written. The narrative should speak for itself. In using a child's voice you are forced not to analyze but merely to tell the story, unembellished.

STUDENT EXAMPLE

The doorbell rings and I know it's Aunt Judith, the old lady I've been hearing about. She's come to visit us from where she lives, San Francisco, which is very far away. It takes almost a whole day to fly to my house from there in an airplane. She's very old, probably around eighty. I'm peeking through the stair railings when my father answers the door. All I can see is a gray coat and some white hair. She must be deaf because my father's voice is loud when he says hello.

My mother calls, "Come down and meet your Aunt Judith." She's holding her aunt's hand and smiling. I come down and stand behind my mother when I say hello. I don't want her to kiss me. She has more wrinkles on her face than I ever saw. She pats my head and says, "So big for five."

My father says he's going to make some tea. My mother and Aunt Judith and I go into the living room and sit down.

"Come here, Emily, and sit by your old aunt," she says, patting the couch next to her.

I feel funny but I go and sit where she says. She smells like bread in the oven.

"Tell Aunt Judith about school," my mother says.

"I'll be in first grade next September," I say.

My father comes in with the teapot on a tray and some cups. I'm too young to drink tea. I tried it once and it tasted like dirt.

My mother and Aunt Judith are talking about people I don't know. My father looks like he doesn't know them either. I'm staring, but Aunt Judith doesn't mind. She has a mouth that sticks out like a fish with hairs over her top lip. Then I say, "You know what Aunt Judith? You have a mustache." I don't make it up; she does have a mustache; it's just like my grandfather's only not quite so bushy. Aunt Judith gets a funny look on her face. She stands up and says, "Where's the bathroom?"

My mother shows her where the bathroom is and when she comes back she tells me that I shouldn't have said that about Aunt Judith's mustache. "But it's true!" I say.

My mother tells me that just because something's true doesn't mean I have to say it out loud. She looks angry.

Aunt Judith stays in the bathroom a very long time. I want to tell Aunt Judith I'm sorry but I don't know how to. Finally, my mother knocks on the bathroom door. "Are you all right, Judith?" Maybe she thinks she's dead or something.

I can hear Aunt Judith's voice but not what she says. My mother says, "She's okay."

My father says, "Big-mouth Emily."

I'm not staying around any more. I go upstairs but not to my room. I sit at the top where I can hear Aunt Judith when she finally comes out of the bathroom.

EMILY HONIG

In probing my childhood (which is the next best to probing one's eternity) I see the awakening of consciousness as a series of spaced flashes, with the intervals between them gradually diminishing until bright blocks of perception are formed, affording memory a slippery hold.

VLADIMIR NABOKOV

23

AN EARLY MEMORY, PART TWO: THE REMINISCENT NARRATOR

Something crucial to remember: The story doesn't exist until you tell it. In other words, whatever its bare bones, it's how you, the writer, put them together that counts. Viewpoint, tone, style, narrative shape, and time distance—all these elements have as much to do with a story as does the basic "plot." A reminiscent narrator remembers something because it has a special, pointed meaning for him. Here is how the adult Frank Conroy writes about his father, who died young. The book is *Stop-Time*.

> And I remember visiting him at one of the rest homes when I was eight. We walked across a sloping lawn and he told me a story, which even then I recognized as a lie, about a man who sat down on the open blade of a penknife embedded in a park bench. (Why, for God's sake would he tell a story like that to his eight-year-old son?)

We draw up out of the well of our unconscious those things that have emotional significance. In contrast to the previous exercise, this one will force you to search—with an adult sensibility—for the underlying "meaning" of the event you simply reported in "An Early Memory, Part One" (p. 64). What have you learned in the interim? What can be gained (or maybe lost) by hindsight?

THE EXERCISE

In no more than two pages, use the incident of "An Early Memory, Part One" and tell it from the vantage point of who you are today, that is, inject it with adult vocabulary, insight, subtlety, and comprehension. For instance, "My father was obviously confused" replaces "funny look." You should change the way the incident is told without altering its structure or meaning. Use the past tense but keep it a first-person narrative. As in the first part of this exercise, try to let the material speak for itself.

THE OBJECTIVE

As in a good many of these exercises, the idea is to empower the writer with the knowledge that he controls the material, and not the other way around. There are countless ways to tell the same story and each way says something a little different, not only about what happened but also about how the teller feels about it. You're the first and last authority; your power—at least in this realm—is unlimited.

STUDENT EXAMPLE

At the age of five I learned how easy it is to wound someone simply by pointing out to them something obvious to everyone else. I think that I forgot this from time to time as I got older but I certainly learned it in a dramatic way.

My mother's Aunt Judith was then in her late eighties—an old but vigorous childless widow who had helped translate the books of Thomas Mann and lived alone in Berkeley, California. She had come East to visit her brother, my mother's father, and was paying a call at our house. I had never met her and was a timid child anyway, so I hung back until she patted the couch beside her and told me to come sit next to her. I could tell by the expression on my mother's face that she was anxious to have Aunt Judith like and approve of me. I think my mother and she had had an unusually close relationship when my mother was young and lived in New York— where Aunt Judith also lived before she moved to the West Coast.

My father offered to make some tea and disappeared into the kitchen. I mainly listened while my mother and Aunt Judith reminisced about people whose names I didn't recognize. But I didn't really mind because I was having such a good time staring at her face. It was a mass of veins and wrinkles—

far more than my grandfather had. And she had a black mustache. If you hadn't seen her clothes or heard her speak you might have thought she was a man.

My father came back with the tea and they all drank, Aunt Judith making slurping noises and seeming to enjoy herself except that she really didn't have any idea how to talk to a child as young as I was. She asked me one question—I think it was about school—and then seemed to forget I was there.

But, as I said before, I didn't mind at all; I was a watcher.

Did I know, at some depth, that I should not say what I then said? To this day I'm not certain. But, with no windup, I suddenly said, "You know what, Aunt Judith? You have a mustache."

Her hand flew to her mouth; she looked as if someone had just pierced her lung with a sharp knife. She stared at me, got up, and said, very quietly, "Anne, will you please tell me where the bathroom is?"

My mother was obviously flustered and led her to the downstairs bathroom.

When she came back my mother tried to explain to me that just because something was true did not mean that you had to say it out loud. On my part, I tried to argue but soon gave up because I felt so bad. My father told me I was a big-mouth.

Aunt Judith stayed in the bathroom for fully fifteen minutes. I think my mother was worried that she had fainted. I knew what she was doing: She was studying herself in the mirror, perhaps seeing this horrible mustache for the first time; it must have been a shock.

They were annoyed at me and embarrassed by what I had done (and I can't say I really blame them. A big child but a tactless one). They were nice enough to let me go upstairs. The truth doesn't carry with it its own protection against pain.

EMILY HONIG

24

THE UNRELIABLE NARRATOR

Yᴏᴜ ᴍᴀʏ ꜰɪɴᴅ ᴛʜᴀᴛ ʏᴏᴜ ᴡᴀɴᴛ ᴛᴏ ᴄʀᴇᴀᴛᴇ ᴀ ᴄʜᴀʀᴀᴄᴛᴇʀ ᴡʜᴏ ꜱᴀʏꜱ one thing and unwittingly reveals another—for example, a teacher who claims to love all her students, even those with "funny, hard-to-pronounce names and weird haircuts." The unreliable narrator—between whose lines the author invites you to read—is a classic fixture in works of fiction. Eudora Welty's narrator in "Why I live at the P.O." is a wonderful example of unreliability. So is the narrator of Ford Madox Ford's *The Good Soldier*.

THE EXERCISE

Using the first person, write a self-deceiving portrait in which the narrator is not the person she thinks she is—either more or less admirable. You must give your readers clues that your narrator is skewing the truth.

THE OBJECTIVE

To create a narrator who unwittingly reveals—through subtle signals of language, details, contradictions, and biases—that his or her judgment of events and people is too subjective to be trusted. The reader must thus discount the version of the story offered by the narrator and try to re-create a more objective one for himself.

STUDENT EXAMPLE

A young girl should stand up straight. That's what I told my daughter-in-law, Ruthie. "Don't slouch," is really what I said,

70

"look proud to be with my son." I must say, I've never seen anyone take such offense at a harmless comment.

"You're always criticizing me," Ruthie said. "First you tell me I don't keep the house clean enough, and then you tell me that I'm not feeding your son."

I have to defend myself, don't I? To begin with, I said, "These things you call criticisms—they aren't. They are helpful suggestions, something one woman can say to another. I never said the house wasn't clean enough, it's just that with two small children, sometimes you get too busy to keep house the way you'd like to." The only reason I mentioned the dust balls under the couch was for the children's sake. And, I certainly didn't say that my son wasn't being fed. I only remarked that he was so skinny, that maybe he didn't have time to eat a good meal because of all the work he has to do, being such a nice man to help his wife the way he does. Really, my daughter-in-law is a good girl. She learns fast. I know her mother—she can't help it that she has some bad habits.

And then my son, Geoff, he feels he should protect his wife, so he says, "Ma, quit ragging on Ruthie. Mind your own business, Ma." I understand how he has to take his wife's side so she doesn't get angry at him. But me and Geoff, we have an understanding. I know he agrees with me, so I'm just helping him out a little by mentioning these things, right? He could have had any girl. He's a nice boy to stay with Ruthie and the kids and I just want her to appreciate what she's got.

HESTER KAPLAN

V: DIALOGUE

Dialogue is, basically, two or more characters talking to each other. It is also an ideal, compact way to advance your story by having one character tell another what's happening—to reveal, admit, incite, accuse, lie, etc.

Furthermore, dialogue is an economical way of defining a character; the way someone speaks—accent, vocabulary, idiom, inflection, etc.—tells us as much about what he is like as his actions do.

Dialogue is never a faithful rendering of the way human beings really speak. At its most poetic it is the iambic pentameter of Shakespeare's plays; at the other end is Mark Twain's Huckleberry Finn using the Mississippi Valley vernacular of the 1840s. Both authors omit the hesitations, repetitions, false starts, meanderings and aborted phrases that make actual human talk so much less compelling. Read a transcript of testimony or of a taped telephone conversation or listen attentively to the next person with whom you have a conversation and you will realize that fictional dialogue is only an approximation of true speech, having been shaped, pointed, and concentrated.

Paradoxically, dialogue is often useful for getting across *what is not said*, what we call the subtext. For instance, if you want to show that someone in a story or novel wants to avoid an unpleasant encounter, you can indicate this by having them talk around the topic uppermost in their mind but never quite touching it. In using dialogue this way, you're asking the reader to read between the lines. This is a tricky maneuver but if you think about how you talk to someone yourself when you're angry at them but don't want to tell them exactly why— by being sarcastic, arch, nitpicky, oversolicitous, etc.—you'll get it right.

It's important, too, to learn when to use direct discourse— *he said, she said*—and when to summarize by indirect discourse. This is partly a matter of what "feels" right and partly of how important the actual words used are to your narrative. For example, forcing character A to answer the phone "Hello," and then having character B say "Hello" back isn't essential, flat, and boring—everyone knows how you answer the phone. Far better to cut to the chase: what did character A learn from B's phone call that moves the story along or tells us something crucial about either or both A and B?

25

SPEECH FLAVOR, OR SOUNDING REAL

from Thalia Selz

Hᴇʀᴇ ᴄᴏᴍᴇs ʏᴏᴜʀ ᴄʜᴀʀᴀᴄᴛᴇʀ. Sʜᴇ's Iʀɪsʜ—Hɪsᴘᴀɴɪᴄ—Vɪᴇᴛɴᴀᴍ-
ese—a Maine congresswoman, a shrimp boatman from Loui-
siana, or a black professor of English in an Ivy League college
who retains traces of her Chicago slum childhood in her
speech. Your character is eager to have the conversation that
the structure of the story demands. Or maybe she wants to tell
the story, as in a first-person narrative. Either way, you want
that speech to have its own flavor, to suggest the character
and background of the person uttering it, without using much
phonetic spelling because it can be hard to read. Characters
in fiction, like real people, have to come out of a context to be
convincing and intriguing—even when that context is imagi-
nary, like postatomic holocaust England in Russell Hoban's
Riddley Walker.

THE EXERCISE

Observe how the following speech fragments convey a sense
of accent or national, regional, race, class, or cultural distinc-
tions mainly through word choice and arrangement. Easily understood foreign words or names can help, too. What do these
fragments suggest about the individual speakers by conveying
the flavor of their speech?

> My mama dead. She die screaming and cussing.
> Aʟɪᴄᴇ Wᴀʟᴋᴇʀ, *The Color Purple*

> " 'I won't keep you,' I says. 'You must get a job for yourself.'
> But, sure, it's worse whenever he gets a job; he drinks it all."
> Jᴀᴍᴇs Jᴏʏᴄᴇ, "Ivy Day in the Committee Room"

All in all, Harry Laines' wedding was one of the worst events in my experience, tragic in society.

NANCY LEMANN, *Lives of the Saints*

"Muy buenos," I said. "Is there an Englishwoman here? I would like to see this English lady."

"Muy buenos. Yes, there is a female English."

ERNEST HEMINGWAY, *The Sun Also Rises*

". . . the working mens one Sunday afternoon taking they only time off. They laying around drinking some moonshine, smoking the hemp, having a cock fight."

PETER LEACH, "The Convict's Tale"

"My own wife is seven years older than me. So what did I suffer?—Nothing. If Rothschild's daughter wants to marry you, would you say on account her age, no?"

BERNARD MALAMUD, "The Magic Barrel"

"Why me?" she rumbled. "It's no trash around here, black or white, that I haven't given to. And break my back to the bone every day working. And do for the church."

FLANNERY O'CONNOR, "Revelation"

"Father says for you to come on and get breakfast," Caddy said. "Father says it's over a half an hour now, and you've got to come this minute."

"I ain't studying no breakfast," Nancy said. "I going to get my sleep out."

WILLIAM FAULKNER, "That Evening Sun"

"Copy our sister-in-law," Brave Orchid instructed. "Make life unbearable for the second wife, and she'll leave. He'll have to build her a second house."

"I wouldn't mind if she stays," said Moon Orchid. "She can comb my hair and keep house. She can wash dishes and serve our meals . . ."

MAXINE HONG KINGSTON, *The Woman Warrior*

Now write five of your own speech fragments.

THE OBJECTIVE

In this case, it is threefold: to help reveal character, to convince your reader by making your dialogue sound credible, and to add variety. Differences in speech aren't just realistic; they're interesting and provocative, and they can give vitality to your story. Speech without flavor is like food without savor.

STUDENT EXAMPLES

"Those dipsticks down at work made Ron my boss. What a kick in the butt, huh?" I smiled even though I didn't want to, but Mary Lou didn't smile back, and I'm thinking if *I* can smile—and I feel like hell—why can't she?

BOB PELTIER, "Making M1s"

"Who you think you're dealin with, boy? Hoot and holler like that at me again, and there'll be a whoopin' you'll never forget."

PETER BAER

I looked at the Pall Mall. I wondered if he smoked them things without filters so me and my friends wouldn't bum them all away. Tobacco don't taste *that* good. I thought 'bout whether I wanted it bad enough to smoke it anyways, decided I did, took a toke. Tasted like burning rubber boots. "Garbage," I said.

TERY GRIFFIN, "Where the Man Belongs"

"Tank you."—"It's *thank* you."—"No *tank* you?"—"No. *Thank* you."—"Oh! Sank you."

CYNTHIA HOLLOBAUGH

26

DIALOGUE IS ALL ART, NOT TALK

Dialogue has a difficult task in that it must simulate real talk at the same time it must artfully waste no words, reveal character, provide tension, and move the story forward. For example, in real life we do answer the telephone with "Hello," followed by an identifying exchange, and perhaps some small talk. Yet rarely do writers use these lines because they are so taken for granted. Today we might say,

> The phone rang. It was George wanting to borrow the jeep. I told him, "Don't bring it back without a full tank of gas."

Dialogue generally goes for the heart of the story, the exchange that matters, the confrontation.

THE EXERCISE

Have a fellow writer do this exercise with you. Make up situations involving two people who disagree about something—for example, two friends who have planned to shoplift something and one is getting cold feet. Or a landlord and a tenant disagree about the terms of a lease. Next, tape your dialogue as you and your friend "act out" the two "roles" in a scene. Don't decide what you're going to say ahead of time. Improvise, through dialogue, as you go along. Then transcribe the dialogue exactly as it was said.

Here is where your writer's ear comes in. Read over the written account of your scene. How much of the original exchange is useful for your story? How much of the dialogue might you summarize? And are there any "perfect" lines that you would keep? Finally try writing the scene using the transcribed dialogue to give shape to the scene. How much of the original dialogue would you keep?

THE OBJECTIVE

To hear and see how real talk is repetitive, disjointed, and boring. At the same time, to train your writer's ear to transform actual speech into carefully crafted dialogue.

THE INVISIBLE SCENE:
INTERSPERSING DIALOGUE WITH ACTION

FLANNERY O'CONNOR, IN HER ESSAY "WRITING SHORT STORIES," says that in beginning stories,

> dialogue frequently proceeds without the assistance of any characters that you can actually see, and uncontained thought leaks out of every corner of the story. The reason is usually that the student is wholly interested in his thoughts and his emotions and not in his dramatic action, and that is he is too lazy or highfalutin to descend to the concrete where fiction operates.

When you are writing a scene in a story, it might help to think of your characters as being onstage. Your reader will want to know what they look like and what the stage setting looks like. Next, your reader will want to have a sense of how your characters move around and interact with the furniture of their stage world—in other words the stage business, body language, or choreography. Characters live in a concrete world and it is your job as a fiction writer to keep them there.

THE EXERCISE

Write a scene in which a character's body, as well as as his mind, is engaged in doing something—stage business. Here are some possibilities:

repairing something
playing solitaire or a game involving other players
doing exercises
painting a canvas or a wall

cutting down a tree
giving someone a haircut

Come up with your own suggestions

Explore how various activities and settings can change what happens within a scene. For example, what happens when characters are planning their honeymoon if they are painting an apartment or one of them is cutting the other's hair. Or what happens when characters are having a confrontation in public—say in a fancy restaurant—rather than in the privacy of their home.

It is also instructive to analyze how a writer you admire handles the interweaving of dialogue and body language. Go through one of your favorite stories and highlight all the body language and choreography. We guarantee this will teach you something.

THE OBJECTIVE

To give concrete life to the scenes our characters inhabit. To understand how action and choreography relate to the objects in the scene and how all of these relate to and help shape dialogue and the engagement of the characters.

28

NOT QUITE A FIGHT

THANK GOD FOR DIALOGUE. DIALOGUE IS ONE OF THE FICTION WRIT-
er's most useful tools. But it's tricky. Good dialogue is not at
all the way human beings speak to each other—it's an approximation. Dialogue takes human speech and renders it con-
densed, highlighted, and pointed. Dialogue is extremely useful
when you want to show what a character is thinking and want
to avoid the leaden "she thought" formulation. Simply bring
on another character and have the two of them hold a conversation. Dialogue reveals character—as anyone who has ever
seen a decent play knows. It is also good for breaking up long
paragraphs and provides an opportunity to use common idi-
oms. The way a character talks—vocabulary, tone, style, and
sense of humor—can tell your readers exactly what you want
them to know in a "showing" way that narrative can only
"tell."

THE EXERCISE

Write a dialogue between two people who know each other,
each taking the opposite side of an issue or problem. This
should be a verbal dance, not a shouting match. The issue you
choose should be something immediate and particular (like
whether to spend money on a vacation or put it in the savings
account) rather than abstract (communism is going down the
tubes). Keep it simple and emotionally close to the two people
involved. The speakers should be equally convincing. That is,
you, the author, can't load the argument on one side or the
other. Make each person distinctive in her oral style, for example, in vocabulary and tone. Keep in mind that the subtext—what the conversation reveals about the speakers'
relationship to each other—is as important as the manifest

text. For example, in the what-shall-we-do-with-the-money conversation the subtext is about which of the two speakers has more power—and is willing to exploit it. Limit: 550 words.

THE OBJECTIVE

To learn to use dialogue to reveal character and human dynamics and to understand that speaking style says as much about a person as her behavior does. Incidentally, you should also recognize that dialogue should not be used for the following: for lengthy exposition, to furnish your stage, as a substitute for action, and as a vehicle for showing off your own vocabulary and education. A false line of dialogue can ruin an entire scene.

STUDENT EXAMPLE

"I'm giving up, Jim," Maria said to her husband. "I'm done, finished. No more doctors, no more tests. The end."

"Maria," Jim said patiently. "I think we should keep trying. You know the doctors say there's still a chance."

"They might say that," Maria said, "but *I* know there isn't. My body just doesn't want to have a baby. You know how there are some places in the city that just can't make a go of it? A restaurant moves in, people line up, and in six months it's gone? Or a new store moves in, and business is great at first, but then customers stop coming and the business folds? Think of it that way, Jim. My body is a low-rent district for good reason."

"God, Maria," Jim said, covering his face, "you know I hate it when you talk like this, when you put yourself down. It's beneath you."

"I'm not putting myself down, Jim. I'm simply stating the fact that I'm not going to get pregnant. And the sooner you admit that, the sooner we can start looking for a baby to adopt."

"No, Maria. We can't adopt. It's not right."

"What do you mean right, Jim?"

"You know what I mean, Maria. Right. Comes from a good family, is healthy, you know, things like that."

"You mean a baby's parents had to go to Yale?"

"You know that's not what I mean, Maria. But here we are, two rich, well-educated, good-looking, smart people, and we could end up with an ugly, stupid baby."

"God forbid, Jim, an ugly baby. Wouldn't look too good at your twenty-fifth reunion, would it?" Maria said.

"You're twisting my words around, Maria, and you know it. You always pretend not to understand what I'm saying. You never just give me what I want."

"What you want? Is that it, Jim?" Maria said. "I knew there was some reason I wasn't getting pregnant. I guess I just don't want it enough."

"Your sarcasm isn't very productive, Maria."

"Neither are we, Jim. That's what we're talking about here, isn't it?"

HESTER KAPLAN

29

TELLING TALK: WHEN TO USE DIALOGUE OR INDIRECT DISCOURSE (SUMMARIZED DIALOGUE)

ONE OF THE MOST IMPORTANT DECISIONS A WRITER MUST MAKE IS whether to use dialogue or to summarize it. Too often dialogue is incorrectly used to provide information that could have been given in indirect discourse. Or else the reader is given the entire scene—for example, the full escalation of an argument—when in fact only the closing lines are important to hear verbatimo.

Summarized dialogue allows the writer to condense speech, set the pace of the scene, reveal attitudes, make judgments, describe the talk, avoid sentimentality, and emphasize crucial lines of actual dialogue.

Study the following passages to learn what summarized dialogue accomplishes. Then transform the summarized dialogue into dialogue to understand why the author chose to condense it.

So this ordinary patrolman drove me home. He kept his eye on the road, but his thoughts were all on me. He said that I would have to think about Mrs. Metzger, lying cold in the ground, for the rest of my life, and that, if he were me, he would probably commit suicide. He said that he expected some relative of Mrs. Metzger would get me sooner or later, when I least expected it—maybe the very next day, or maybe when I was a man, full of hopes and good prospects, and with a family of my own. Whoever did it, he said, would probably want me to suffer some.

I would have been too addled, too close to death, to get his name, if he hadn't insisted that I learn it. It was Anthony Squires, and he said it was important that I commit it to memory, since I would undoubtedly want to make a complaint about him, since policemen were expected to speak politely at all times, and that, before he got me home, he was going to call me a little Nazi cocksucker and a dab of catshit and he hadn't decided what all yet.

KURT VONNEGUT, JR., *Deadeye Dick*

They talked of things that had happened to them—to them!—these past ten years. I waited in vain to hear my name on my wife's sweet lips: "And then my dear husband came into my life"—something like that. But I heard nothing of the sort. More talk of Robert. Robert had done a little of everything, it seemed, a regular blind jack-of-all-trades. But most recently he and his wife had had an Amway distributorship, from which, I gathered, they'd earned their living, such as it was. The blind man was also a ham operator. He talked in his loud voice about conversations he'd had with fellow operators in Guam, in the Philippines, in Alaska, and even in Tahiti. He said he'd have a lot of friends there if he ever wanted to go visit those places. From time to time, he'd turn his blind face toward me, put his hand under his beard, ask me something. How long had I been in my present position: (Three years.) Did I like my work? (I didn't.) Was I going to stay with it? (What were my options?) Finally, when I thought he was beginning to run down, I got up and turned on the TV.

RAYMOND CARVER, "Cathedral"

She sits in the visitor's chair beside the raised bed, while Auntie Muriel, wearing an ice-blue bed-jacket, cranked up and propped up, complains. They put extra chlorine in the water here, she can taste it. She can remember when water was water but she doesn't suppose Elizabeth can tell the difference. At first she could not get a private room. Can Elizabeth imagine? She had to share a room, share one, with a terrible old woman who wheezed at night. Auntie Muriel is convinced the woman was dying. She could hardly get any sleep. And now that she's finally here in her private room, no one pays any attention to her. She has to ring and ring, three times even, before the nurse will come. They all read detective novels, she's seen them. The night nurse is from the West Indies. The food is atrocious. She cannot tolerate beets, she always ticks the other vegetables on the menu but they bring beets. Sometimes Auntie Muriel thinks they do things like this to her on purpose. She will speak to Doctor MacFadden, tomorrow. If she has to stay here for a little rest and some tests, which is what he says, the least he can do is make sure she's comfortable. She's never been sick a day in her life, there's nothing really wrong with her now, she isn't used to hospitals.

Elizabeth thinks this may be true.

MARGARET ATWOOD, *Life Before Man*

She talked for forty minutes straight. There seemed to be less connection between her ideas, but the ideas themselves were, as the dictionary would say, fabulous. She said she had heard of a huge jewel, in what she called the Antipodes, that was so brilliant that when the light shone into it at a certain angle it would blind whoever was looking at its center. She said that the biggest diamond in the world was cursed and had killed everyone who owned it, and that by a trick of fate it was called the Hope diamond. Diamonds are magic, she said, and this is why women wear them on their fingers as a sign of the magic of womanhood. Men have strength, Miss Ferenczi said, but no true magic. That is why men fall in love with women but women do not fall in love with men: they just love being loved. George Washington had died because of a mistake he made about a diamond.

CHARLES BAXTER, "Gryphon"

EXERCISE

Highlight the dialogue in a story by a writer you admire. Then determine how much dialogue is summarized rather than presented in quotation marks.

Next, set up a situation in which one character is going on and on about something—complaining about grades, arguing with a spouse about the children, or recounting an accident to a friend. Summarize the dialogue, occasionally interspersing it with comments and stage directions.

OBJECTIVE

To understand what summarized dialogue accomplishes and how it affects tone, pace, and the shaping of a scene.

STUDENT EXAMPLES

He told me the flypaper was on sale and that even if it wasn't
I could walk around town and still not find a cheaper brand.
I nodded in agreement but said that what I wanted was a bug
light, not flypaper. He rolled his eyes and demanded to know
exactly how much I knew about bug lights. Before I could tell
him, he pointed his finger at me and explained that the voltage
requirements were incredible. A modest bug zapper would
cost me five times over what I paid for it during one wet Torville spring and one hot Torville summer. Then there were the
outages, which occurred at least twice a summer when everyone was using air-conditioning. No bug protection then, he
said. And there was the sheer cumbersomeness of the things.
He clapped his hand on my shoulder and brought his mouth
close to my ear and said, "They're all made by the Japs. Think
what you're doing to this country."

ALEXANDER INGLE

No one could be certain whether Kadi had died by accident
or by her own design, yet it was much debated over smoky
fires far into the humid West African night, in the manner
peculiar to the Fula people. Adulai Embalo, speaker for the
village elders, cited the evidence indicating an accident: that
Kadi had often slipped at the muddy, sloping edge of the well
as she drew water; that she had been up that morning before
first light and could not have seen clearly where the bucket-
ropes of other women had worn a new incline at the lip of the
well; and that her sandals were found nearby, but not her
enormous tin washbasin, suggesting that she had been mount-
ing the heavy load on her head when her wet bare feet lost
their hold on the slick clay.

The others listened respectfully to this, and paused in silence to consider it in the glow of the dying coals. Mamadu
then proposed the facts that suggested Kadi had taken her
own life: that she had quarreled with her husband Demba the
night before; that she had been ashamed not to have con-
ceived since her third miscarriage the previous rainy season;
and that her rice plot had been damaged by wandering cattle
so that her harvest would be less than half of what she and
Demba needed toward the purchase of medicine to fertilize
her womb, or toward the purchase of a second wife for
Demba. But little could be done about Kadi now, except to

discuss and turn over each point cited by the speakers, which is what the other village elders did as the fire slowly died, savoring the joy of conversation in the arcane Fulani of older men.

CAMERON MACAULEY, "The Woman at the Well"

Recently, I was engaged in a profoundly meaningful conversation in one corner of a large common room. In the corner opposite somebody was trying to conduct some silly group discussion. Presently, a young man strode briskly across the floor and tapped me on the shoulder. "Can you try and keep it down?" he said. "You can't imagine how your voice carries." . . . *It carries.* Yes, that's the idea, isn't it? You say what you have to say the way you have to say it and hope to hell you're bothering somebody.

SHARON SHEEHE STARK, *Other Voices*

VI: PLOT

Except for the first two exercises in this section, most have as much to do with characterization as with plot. When we completed our first draft of *What If?*, plot was entirely missing from the table of contents. We did have exercises that fit this category, but we had placed them elsewhere. Then someone said, "Where's plot?" Well it's here. But for us it comes strongly attached to characterization.

Hemingway and William Kennedy feel the same way. In a *Paris Review* interview, Kennedy says,

> Hemingway's line was that everything changes as it moves; and that that is what makes the movement that makes the story. Once you let a character speak or act you now know that he acts this way and no other. You dwell on why this is so and you move forward to the next page. This is my method. I'm not interested in formulating a plot to which characters are added like ribbons on a prize cow. The character is the key and when he does something which is new, something you didn't know about or expect, then the story percolates. If I knew, at the beginning, how the book was going to end, I would probably never finish.

So get to know your characters by placing them in a situation and then discover what happens. Our exercise "What If?" is designed to provide you with several organic ways to move your story forward toward complication and resolution. Always, always with character in motion. In her book, *Mystery and Manners*, Flannery O'Connor recalls lending some stories to a neighbor who when she gave them back said, "Well, them stories just gone and shown you how some folks *would* do." And O'Connor says, "I thought to myself that that was right; when you write stories, you have to be content to start exactly there—showing how some specific folks *will* do, *will* do in spite of everything." And that doing is plot.

30

THREE BY THREE

from William Melvin Kelley

W<small>E ALL KNOW THE CLASSIC STORY DESCRIPTION</small>: B<small>OY MEETS GIRL</small>. Boy loses girl. Boy gets girl. What is implied in those three three-word sentences is that a story has a beginning, a middle, and an end. For example, here is Cinderella:

Cinderella can't go.
She goes anyway.
Cinderella gets Prince.

And here is the Pied Piper:

Man lures rats.
People won't pay.
Man takes children.

Although this story structure won't work for more complicated stories, it is surprising how often it does work, and how full these stories can be.

THE EXERCISE

Break your story idea down into three sentences of three words each. That will give you a beginning, a middle, and an end and help you understand the architecture of the work. By having to choose three verbs, you'll be forcing yourself to consider the three parts of the action.

THE OBJECTIVE

To see if your story, like a good stool, has three legs to stand on.

93

31

THE SKELETON

THE SIMPLEST STORIES ARE FAIRY TALES AND MYTHS IN WHICH A central character—who is on some sort of quest or journey—is continually on stage and secondary characters only appear to assist or thwart her. This is what we call a "skeleton" story—you can see its bones. There are no subtleties, motivation is a given, emotions are unanalyzed, and the narrative proceeds in a linear way. In the skeleton the world and its people are viewed in morally black-and-white terms. The temptation to stray will be almost irresistible but if you do, you will drag your reader into thickets of subplots and gangs of minor characters. (The following exercise is based on a suggestion of folklorist Lawrence Millman.)

THE EXERCISE

Write a linear story, in which a strong main character is on a quest for something important and specific (e.g., a shelter for the baby, medicine for a sick mother, or the key to the storehouse where a tyrant has locked away all the grain from a starving populace). The object is a given—don't explain its importance. The main character starts acting immediately. She then meets a (specific) obstacle; finally she triumphs over the obstacle by means of a magic or supernatural element that comes from the outside (like Dorothy's red shoes in *The Wizard of Oz*). You may introduce minor characters but the narrative should never abandon your main character. This story should be told through action and dialogue. Limit: 550 words.

THE OBJECTIVE

Like a medical student who must learn the names and location of human bones before going on to more complex systems, a beginning writer must be able to handle and control basic plot before moving on to more subtle elements like motivation, subtext, and ambiguity. Many of the greatest novels incorporate a quest (*Moby Dick*), a journey (*David Copperfield*), and triumph over an obstacle (*The Old Man and the Sea*). These works also concentrate on one protagonist and end, if not happily, at least on an emotionally satisfying note of resolution.

STUDENT EXAMPLE

The Nanny—A Fairy Tale

There was once a young woman named Mia who wanted a baby. The urge to produce another life in her own body hit suddenly, like a squall or a virus. Before this, she hadn't particularly liked children. She never made eyes at babies on buses, and usually asked for another table when seated near children in restaurants. She tolerated the children of friends but never played with them the way some guests did. Yet now, without warning, she longed for an infant to nurse, to rock, to carry like a prize in a bundle strapped to her chest. She could imagine exactly the shape and the weight of a baby in her arms.

"A baby?" said her husband, Beau. "You don't know a diaper from a linen handkerchief. Babies are loud, they're smelly, and they cramp your sex life. We're fine as we are."

Mia worked on Beau. Walking through the park she'd point out babies sleeping like sacks in strollers, crowing and waving from backpacks, or toddling on creased legs. "Let's eat Chinese tonight," Beau said. If only Mia could find the secret crack in his heart, the place where the gates would swing open when the magic words were said, letting the idea of their own baby enter like the children of Hamlin.

Mia took to sitting on playground benches, thinking. She could leave Beau and find a man who shared her longing. But she loved the fullness of his laugh, the way he sang as he cooked, the curls behind his ears when his haircut was overdue. She knew she'd miss the stories he read her from the morning paper and the way he kneaded her shoulders after work. Maybe she could trick him, pretend her cycle had become unpredictable, blame nature. But she'd never been able to lie well, not even to her mother.

One day as Mia sat on a bench near a wading pool, a gray-haired nanny sat down beside her, starched uniform gleaming in the sun. "Have any children?" she asked, starting to knit. Mia smiled and shook her head. "Too bad. You'd like a child, wouldn't you? Not married? Men are hard to find these days, they say."

Though partly put off by the nanny's presumptuousness, Mia shared her problem. "My husband doesn't want children. At least not yet."

"Stalled adolescence," the nanny diagnosed. "See it more and more. Want a solution?" Without waiting for an answer, she pulled a pomegranate out of her knitting bag. "Serve him this for dessert tonight and for the next two nights and have some for yourself, too. Be sure he sucks the sweet red part, and doesn't eat the seeds. If he balks, tell him it's better than kiwi."

Mia did as she was told, carefully watching Beau savor the sharp sweet taste and spitting the seeds on his plate. She was so preoccupied that she dripped the juice down the front of her blouse. At first Mia noticed no change in her husband. But on the third day, while sipping cappuccino in an intimate Italian restaurant, he said, "What the hell. You want a baby? What are we waiting for?" And Beau took Mia home to bed.

Months later, her stomach as full as a spinnaker, Mia sat again on the bench near the wading pool, resting her legs. The nanny sat down next to her as she had before, uniform crisp, oxfords firmly tied. Eyeing Mia's belly with a smile, she pulled out her knitting and said, "Looking for a nursemaid?"

CHRISTINE MCDONNELL

32

FROM SITUATION TO PLOT

THINKING TOO HARD ABOUT PLOT, AT THE EXPENSE OF CHARACTER, is usually a mistake. And it is important to examine how the two elements of fiction interact most effectively. In their book, *Technique in Fiction,* Robie Macauley and George Lanning suggest that Heracleitus's observation "character is destiny" should be "written on the wall of every novelist's study." Then they go on to say that this is only half of the dynamics of plot, that a given situation is the other half. How a particular character deals with the circumstances of that situation and chooses to act or not act moves the story forward into plot.

Macauley and Lanning suggest thinking of plot in these terms: In the beginning you present a particular character in a situation. The situation should have opposing forces and alternatives. And your central character should have choices—ways of acting or not acting. The situation should evolve from its original elements. It should grow more complicated, more grave, and finally reach a point of crisis. Thereafter follows the resolution of the crisis and the story. Almost always things will have changed.

Consider how writers have placed certain characters in a situation and set them in motion, from which point they move forward, driven by the force of their own personalities: Isabella Archer in Henry James's *Portrait of a Lady,* Humbert Humbert in Vladimir Nabokov's *Lolita,* Hester Prynne in Nathaniel Hawthorne's *The Scarlet Letter,* and Yossarian in Joseph Heller's *Catch-22.*

THE EXERCISE

In a few sentences, create a specific character in a specific situation. Complicate his life with opposing forces and alternatives within that situation. Ask, Given the situation, what would my character want? What would my character do? How would he act or react? How will those actions propel the story toward a point of crisis and a final resolution?

Practice creating characters involved with specific situations. Then outline miniplots for how you would complicate their situations and move them toward an ending. Keep this outline brief.

THE OBJECTIVE

To understand how the most effective plots are those driven by character. To see how a character within the given of any situation creates his own destiny.

33

WHAT IF? HOW TO DEVELOP
AND FINISH STORIES

Wʀɪᴛᴇʀs ꜱᴏᴍᴇᴛɪᴍᴇꜱ ʜᴀᴠᴇ ꜱᴛᴏʀʏ ʙʟᴏᴄᴋꜱ—ᴛʜᴇʏ ʙᴇɢɪɴ ᴀ ꜱᴛᴏʀʏ easily enough, but then they run into trouble when they try to finish it. Well, one possible answer is that some stories don't have enough forward motion to become a successful story—and these should be abandoned. On the other hand, many story beginnings just need to be examined and explored for their inherent possibilities.

THE EXERCISE

Look in your files for a story that seems stuck, a story that has a story block. Next, write at the top of a separate sheet of paper the two words *What If*. Now write five ways of continuing the story, not ending the story, but continuing the story to the next event, scene, etc. Let your imagination go wild. Loosen up your thinking about the events in the story. Your what if's can be as diverse as your imagination can make them. More than likely, and this has proved true through years of teaching and writing, one of the what if's will feel right, organic, to your story and that is the direction in which you should go. Sometimes you will have to do several groups of what if's per story, but that's okay as long as they keep you moving forward.

THE OBJECTIVE

To illustrate that most story beginnings and situations have within them the seeds of the middle and end. You just have to allow your imagination enough range to discover what works.

STUDENT EXAMPLE

One writer began a story about a young boy, Paul, who shop-lifts with a cousin. The story opens when they take something more expensive than they have ever taken before. This raises the stakes immediately. After writing a superb opening scene of two and a half pages, the writer didn't know where to go with the story. Below are her five what if's? for this beginning.

1. Paul decides to admit to shoplifting, but hopes not to implicate his cousin.
2. Paul is excited by shoplifting something more expensive, and talks his cousin into going back again soon.
3. The store security guard notices their theft and decides to set a trap. (Involves some point-of-view issues.)
4. Paul feels brave now and steals something from his step-father—something Paul has wanted for a long time.
5. There is a time shift to five years later when Paul commits a major burglary.

The writer continued the story with the fourth idea because she felt it was a more interesting and complex development of Paul's situation. If she hadn't explored several alternatives, she might not have gotten to this story line.

Writer's block is only a failure of the ego.   NORMAN MAILER

34

MAGNIFYING CONFLICT

from David Ray

Low-energy writing has, in some circles, become fashionable, but it will probably not remain so for very long. Great fiction is tense with conflict—between characters, within characters, between characters and forces opposing them. We need only think of Ernest Pontifex's struggles with his father in the Victorian classic *The Way of All Flesh* or the custody battle of *Kramer vs. Kramer* or Raskolnikov's struggle between his fixation on murder and his impulse to love and remain loyal to his family and its values in *Crime and Punishment*—or more accurately, his struggle between sanity and insanity. We might recall the heroine of *Pamela*, struggling against the wiles of her employer-seducer. Or we might think of Huck Finn, in his perplexity and struggle against the racism he's been taught and his more trustworthy intuition and loyalty to his friend Jim, a runaway slave. In *Moby Dick* there is conflict on many levels, but primarily between hunter and hunted, malefic force and the innocent violence of nature. Any solid work of fiction will provide ready examples. The Japanese poet Kobayashi Issa found a storm of raging conflict even within a dewdrop, the most peaceful thing he could find in nature when he sought a retreat from his grief. The writer who loses touch with his responsibility to energize his fiction with conflict will probably have a very limited or temporary audience.

THE EXERCISE

Take a story you have completed and go through it and intensify the conflict, magnifying the tension and shrillness at every turn, even to the point of absurdity or hyperbole. Add stress wherever possible, both between characters and within them as individuals. Exaggerate the obstacles they face. Be extreme.

THE OBJECTIVE

To create an awareness of the need for a high level of tension while encouraging a healthy regard for how easily it can become excessive. This exercise is not meant to "improve" the story, although it often provokes new and more dynamic descriptions and dialogue. It raises the writer's consciousness about the need for conflict in fiction.

> I guarantee you that no modern story scheme, even plotlessness, will give a reader genuine satisfaction, unless one of those old-fashioned plots is smuggled in somewhere. I don't praise plots as accurate representations of life, but as ways to keep readers reading. When I used to teach creative writing, I would tell students to make their characters want something right away even if it's only a glass of water. Characters paralyzed by the meaninglessness of modern life still have to drink water from time to time. One of my students wrote a story about a nun who got a piece of dental floss stuck between her lower left molars, and who couldn't get it out all day long. I thought that was wonderful. The story dealt with issues a lot more important than dental floss, but what kept readers going was anxiety about when the dental floss would finally be removed. Nobody could read that story without fishing around in his mouth with a finger.
> KURT VONNEGUT, JR., *Paris Review* interview

35

THE STORY MACHINE

from Perry Glasser

Bᴇɢɪɴɴɪɴɢ ᴡʀɪᴛᴇʀs ꜰʀᴇQᴜᴇɴᴛʟʏ ʙᴇʟɪᴇᴠᴇ "ᴛʜᴇʀᴇ ɪs ɴᴏᴛʜɪɴɢ ᴛᴏ write about" or that "all stories have been told." The "Story Machine" is a heuristic device that mimics what many psychological studies have identified as the chief mechanism of creativity—the juxtaposition of two familiar notions so they are perceived as a single, new notion.

THE EXERCISE

On each of five 3-×-5 index cards, print a vocational label, for example, dentist, truck driver, or fashion model. On each of a second set of index cards, write a mildly strange or unusual behavior. The mistakes here are to be too mundane (brush teeth, clean car) or to be too melodramatic (strangled her lover, drove his flaming truck through the prison walls). Somewhere between lies the quirk of the odd that is interesting: set free the parakeet, pick loose the tennis racket strings, or sew closed his sweater sleeves. Some writers will keep their cards filed for use again and again, and will add to the original pack over time as interesting vocations or actions suggest themselves.

Shuffle each pack of cards (*not* together) and turn over the first pair. The writer may now ask the following question: "Why did Card A do Card B?" "Why did the fashion model pick loose the tennis racket strings?" "Why did the dentist set free the parakeet?" The writer may continue flipping cards until a satisfactory pairing is discovered. If no satisfactory pair develops, reshuffle the cards and repeat the procedure. If you have ten cards in each pack you will have 100 possible pairings; twelve cards per pack will yield 144 pairings.

Bear in mind that the event suggested by the Story Machine should be thought of as the *last* scene of a story. Supply motive for the odd behavior. Supply setting. Supply a conflict that might be resolved by this behavior. Imagine a scene prior to the final scene that demonstrates the severity of the conflict. Imagine a scene that demonstrates the initial difficulty.

This exercise may easily be adapted for a class. Instead of shuffling, students pass cards one way and then another so that no student is left with any of her original cards. The liberating outcome is that if the new pair lacks all resonance for a student, the student has no emotional investment in the product of the Story Machine. No one has made a mistake or performed badly, just some bad luck has occurred. Class discussions of motive and structure can be lively.

THE OBJECTIVE

Retrograde plotting is often a revelation to the beginning writer who has again and again found herself staring off into the space above the typewriter and asking "Now what happens?" Writing toward a conclusion for some writers is easier than exploring the consequences of an imagined premise. One more easily discovers the beginnings of things if one knows the ending. That the Story Machine requires vocational labels gives students insight to the rudiments of characterization, as such labels suggest education levels and socioeconomic status.

STUDENT EXAMPLE

This student drew three situation cards: (1) A computer salesman auditions for a local cooking show, (2) a drug dealer begins work at a homeless shelter, and (3) a teacher sets out to make a three-dimensional map of the city. She chose the computer salesman.

> Marlon has always wondered about the tiny veins that make up romaine lettuce. He is awed that they all build on one another like the networks of minuscule computer bits, pushing information through so many little channels to the ultimate source. Maybe the romaine is packed full of knowledge too.

104

Lettuce knowledge for other green and leafy vegetables. User friendly.

Marlon's lettuce is to be used as a frame for his star, the elaborate star baby, Seven Cherry Frozen Aspic Salad. The romaine will serve its function, dying prettily across his best china, a bit of standard greenery. His most basic ingredient.

If he wins over the others auditioning today, Marlon will be "Mr. Noon Day Chef," the seventh Channel 7 cook to premiere on "Noon Potpourri." He likes the number seven. Lucky. Marlon needs this job because of layoffs at Computer World's Westgate Mall office where he worked as salesman and chief technician.

Marlon paints his lettuce carefully with two parts Johnson Wax and just a bit of liquid Crisco. Polishing lettuce is a trick he picked up in *Draping Delectables*, a technical photography book he found at a used-book store. His lettuce will never see the inside of anyone's mouth. It will simply make mouths water. Powerful mouths who dominate the studios at Channel 7.

KARLA HORNER

36
PLOT POTENTIAL

THE MAIN THING TO KEEP IN MIND AS YOU'RE DOING PLOT IS THAT *you're the boss* and not the other way around. It's your story, and you have an infinite number of choices. As a creator of fiction, you should feel supremely at ease in the role of story-teller.

THE EXERCISE

Write five mini-stories (limit: 200 words each) to account for a single event or set of circumstances, such as a man and woman standing on a city sidewalk, hailing a cab. Each story should be different—in characters, plot, and theme—from the others.

THE OBJECTIVE

To loosen the bonds that shackle you to a single, immutable version; to underscore the fact that plot is not preordained but something you can control and manipulate at will, like the strings of a marionette; and to demonstrate once more that there are many ways to skin a cat.

STUDENT EXAMPLE

    1. At 2:00 in the afternoon, John, a forty-four-year-old man in a business suit, and Dawn, a twenty-two-year-old woman in a tight skirt and high heels, came out of the Hancock Building. While John stood in the street trying to hail a cab, Dawn stayed on the sidewalk, sobbed, and blew her nose. When John finally managed to get a cab, he helped Dawn in and then got in next to her. John is Dawn's boss and she is his secretary. At 1:45 she'd gotten a call from the hospital; her mother had

a heart attack and was in intensive care. When Dawn went in to tell John why she had to leave so suddenly, he looked as though it was his mother who was in the hospital. Dawn could not understand why he was so concerned, why he was getting a cab for her, and now going with her to the hospital. He'd never been very nice to Dawn or interested in getting to know her and this show of sympathy was out of character. John held Dawn's hand in the cab and said, "Oh God, oh God." And he wondered how he was going to tell Dawn that he was her mother's lover, that they'd fallen in love the night Dawn brought her mother to the company Christmas party.

2. As usual, Pauline had been totally humiliated by her father, and now he was making a fool of himself trying to hail a cab. Pauline thought that if she stood on the sidewalk and looked like she was waiting for someone, no one would connect her with her father. He'd insisted on coming to her interview with her. He insisted on sitting in the waiting room while she was in with the personnel director, and he pestered the receptionist with stories about how cute Pauline had been as a child and how smart she was as an adult. Pauline knew he did it with good intentions—he wanted her to be safe in the city, but it was driving her crazy. As he flailed his arms and tried to whistle down a cab, she took a few steps backward, and then ran. When she reached the subway station, she decided to ride to the end of the line.

3. Maggie hated the city, the people in it, the noise, the dirt, and especially that man who had stepped out in front of her and was trying to flag down the cab she had been waiting for. When a cab finally pulled up and he put his hand on the door, she bounded off the sidewalk and banged him so hard with her hip that he fell to the street. "Get your own cab, buster."

"Maggie?" he said, still on the ground. "Maggie Pillbox? Is that you?"

"Wow," she said. "It's you, Doctor Pantry. Gosh, if I'd known it was you, I never would have hit you so hard."

"Still hostile, eh?" he said. Doctor Pantry had been Maggie's psychiatrist. She helped him up, and for the next fifty minutes, they stood on the sidewalk, Doctor Pantry listening carefully and taking notes as Maggie told him all her life's woes.

4. The man and woman trying to hail down a cab, the ones dressed like an insurance salesman and his secretary, had just pulled off their greatest crime to date. It wasn't the big time and they knew it, but eleven wallets, a watch, and a solar calculator weren't bad for five minutes' work. Once in the cab, they put the loot on the seat and started going through it, unaware that the cabdriver was watching in his rearview mirror. The woman talked about how they could finally afford Cindy's braces. The man said he could now pay the rent, and the cabdriver took them on a circuitous route to the police station.

5. Joe had been driving a cab for only two weeks and still found the job intoxicating. He liked best trying to figure out what each person was like before they got into his cab. He'd readily admit that he was usually wrong about people. He'd thought the couple he'd picked up that morning was going to scream at each other, but they were silent and held hands. His last fare had turned out to be a transvestite so convincing that he'd almost asked him/her out on a date. Now this couple, the man in the three-piece suit waving him down and the much younger woman on the sidewalk, worked together and were lovers dying to get away for an afternoon of hot passion. Why else the unlikely pair? "Forest Lawn Mortuary," the man said as he got into the car. "And step on it. We don't want to be late."

TERRY FRENCH

VII: STORY ELEMENTS AS A GIVEN

Wᴀɪᴛᴇʀꜱ ɢᴇᴛ ᴛʜᴇɪʀ ɪᴅᴇᴀꜱ ꜰᴏʀ ꜱᴛᴏʀɪᴇꜱ ᴏʀ ɴᴏᴠᴇʟꜱ ꜰʀᴏᴍ ɪɴꜱɪᴅᴇ their heads, from memory, from what they see and hear around them—including the daily newspaper, the tragedy next door, and the overheard conversation. Some writers start with a powerful image, an imagined character who just stands there waiting to have a story woven around her. Other writers start with a situation (e.g., a person taking a shower hearing a strange noise beyond the bathroom door). Although we don't especially endorse it, many writers begin with an abstraction—injustice, war, divorce, child abuse, etc.—and proceed to make up the story and characters that dramatize the idea.

The exercises in this section are here mainly to help the beginning writer recognize effective fictional triggers. Here is a situation—now compose a story growing directly out of it. While some of these triggers are general (e.g., "Sunday") others are quite specific and one ("Stranger than Truth") requires the writer to deal with an "impossible" situation. In other words, they are imagination stretchers and should help writers who feel they "don't know what to write about" or how to recognize fictional potential. It's all out there, floating free, waiting for you to pull it down and anchor it.

37

SUNDAY: DISCOVERING
EMOTIONAL TRIGGERS

MOST OF THE TIME IT DOESN'T MATTER ON WHAT DAY OF THE WEEK you set your action—unless it's a Sunday (remember the movie *Sunday Bloody Sunday?*). Most people feel at loose ends on this day, even those who spend the morning in church. Instead of using the freedom wisely, a lot of us tend to overdo it— overeat, oversleep, overreact. Sundays bring out the worst in people. Children grow anxious as the weekend draws to a close and they realize they haven't done their homework. During football season, another possible area of tension opens up. Then there is the obligatory trip to grandma and grandpa's house for a large heavy meal and some equally heavy recriminations. Things happen on Sundays that wouldn't happen on weekdays. So if you want to examine domestic dynamics close up, set some action on a Sunday and let her rip.

THE EXERCISE

Title it "Sunday." Write 550 words.

THE OBJECTIVE

Certain words and ideas, such as *retirement, in-laws, boss,* and *fraud,* serve as triggers for stories or scenes in fiction. *Sunday* is one of these. Try to think of others.

STUDENT EXAMPLE

On Sunday mornings, walking to the bathroom, I'd be treated to the sight of my roommate, Abby, in bed with a man, yet another man I didn't recognize. Every Sunday, I'd tell myself I needed to get my own apartment, or at least install some doors in this one. I used to love Sundays before Abby moved in. I'd sit in the sunny spot in the kitchen and drink cup after cup of coffee. I'd read the newspaper—first travel, then arts, weddings, the news—and then my mother would call. We'd talk about Sundays that we'd spent together—going to the planetarium, buying bras, cooking barley. Sundays, I didn't touch my students' papers I'd brought home. I didn't get dressed until 11:00 A.M. I didn't mind feeling lonely.

Now, when I was halfway through the arts section, a shirtless man came into the kitchen. I pulled my robe tighter.

"Geez, I hate Sundays," he said. "They're endless. Give me a Saturday night any day. Hey, I'm Stan," he said, putting out I hand. I shook it. Abby trailed in after him.

"Hi, gorgeous," she said to me. "Met Stan?"

"Sure did," I said, smiling and turning back to the paper. Go away, I thought. Go back to bed. Leave me to my Sunday. The phone rang, and shirtless Stan twisted to pick it up.

"Good morning," he said. "Oh. . . . It's for you," he said, handing me the phone.

"Her mother," Abby said. "Every Sunday. Kind of like church, I guess."

"No, Mom," I whispered into the phone that I'd dragged out into the hall. "No, Mom. That was not my boyfriend. . . . No, he's not a burglar. . . . No, I don't know who he is. . . . No, I don't let strange men into my apartment at all hours." And on it went. My head throbbed.

When I got off the phone, I went back into the kitchen. Stan was sitting in my chair. Abby was sitting on Stan's lap twirling his chest hairs.

"Hey, gorgeous," Abby said. "We're going to grab a bagel and then go to the planetarium. Half-price on Sundays. Want to come?"

"Better than sitting around here moping," Stan said. "Ouch. Stop pulling my hairs." He slapped Abby's hand away.

HESTER KAPLAN

38

FIVE DIFFERENT VERSIONS: AND NOT ONE IS A LIE

W<small>E TELL STORIES EVERY DAY OF OUR LIVES. BUT *HOW* WE TELL THE</small> story is often determined by who we are telling the story to. Think of the range of people in one's life—parents, spouse, children, friends, lovers, priests, rabbis, in-laws, social workers, parole officers (come on—use your imagination), doctors, claims adjusters, lawyers, judges, juries, therapists, talk-show hosts, astrologers—the list goes on and on. And as we tell these people our story, we add or subtract, exaggerate or play down, tolerate or condemn, depending on the identity of the person to whom we are telling our tale.

THE EXERCISE

Here is the situation: You have just come out of the movie theater around seven in the evening and you are mugged—a person asks for your money, then knocks you to the ground before running away. Or make up your own situation.

Next, pretend you are telling the account of this event to five different people:

you mother
your best friend
your girlfriend or boyfriend (or wife or husband)
a therapist
a police officer

THE OBJECTIVE

To become conscious of how we shape and shade the stories that we tell to each other according to the listener. Your characters also tell stories to each other and make selections about content according to whom they are telling the story, the effect they want the story to have, and the response they want to elicit from the listener. A lot of dialogue in fiction, in real life, is story telling—and there is always the story listener who is as important to the tale as the tale itself.

STUDENT EXAMPLE

Telling my mother
So I'd been to the bathroom 'cause I knew I wouldn't get to go before I made it home and no, I wasn't wearing my black mini! You don't wear leather in early autumn. Anyway, I'd asked this guy—some kid from school—what time it was and he told me 7:10. Don't worry. He wasn't the mugger—I did not ask the mugger the time. It was Johnny Something Or Other from my morning Lit. 121. Anyway, I'm just walking down the sidewalk, heading for the car and it happened. Johnny Whozit must have heard it. He's a big kid, probably a football player or something, and that's all I could think about there, sitting sprawled all over the ground. That kid could've helped me out.

Telling my best friend
After that last scene where Sonny Bono's wife's hair blows up and the fat girl gets to dance, I decided to just go ahead and leave early. I took a detour by the john and left out the side door, stopping just long enough to remind this student of mine about something. I wasn't out that door five minutes when I got a whiff of the nastiest smell, something like urine and chocolate all mixed together. And it kinda came on me hard and I lost it, I think, just about then. Next, I felt this thing take ahold of my purse, straightaway, lift it off my arm. And then I sat on the ground trying to remember seeing anybody at all.

Telling my boyfriend
Listen, I have never, not once, taken anything so hard. They found me sitting on the sidewalk in front of the Tivoli, my dress up around my bottom, crying, you know. Just out of my head. The policeman told me I was going to have to calm down, tell him some facts. But I couldn't even remember what film I'd been to. (I'd gone to *Hairspray* again for the third time. I

114

know you think that's silly, but I've got this thing about John Waters.) I don't remember a thing past losing my pocketbook. You'd think we were in New York City or something.

Telling my therapist
I have this thing about smells. Dirty smells. Like for instance, my mom tells the story how I'd whip off my diapers the very second they filled up, and well, that's sort of the way I am today. And you can imagine how I felt when this dirty, stinking body—and that's all I can recall about it—pulls into my personal space and attacks. All I could think about was: I am going to get sick, right here, right in front of all Broad Street.

Telling a police officer
I was just minding my business, leaving a little early. School tomorrow. I teach, you know, and he must have come out from one of those cars over there because I didn't see him in the building. He was real big, lots of muscles. I didn't get a good look at his face, but he was dressed like a street person and smelled like one. Strong, you know, in more ways than one.

KARLA HORNER

39

ACCOUNTING: HOW DID
WE GET HERE?

In her wonderful essay "Mr. Bennett and Mrs. Brown" Virginia Woolf talks about her sources of inspiration. She writes, "I believe that all novels begin with an old lady in the corner opposite" [in the train]. That is, the moment she sees a stranger she begins to make up a story about her. When you try this you'll find that some of your stories lead nowhere; others keep on growing. Most experienced fiction writers do this constantly—always making up who that person is and why he's sitting there in the rain. Or what those two people are talking about while waiting in line to buy their tickets. If you don't already have this habit, cultivate it. Start accounting for things, explaining who, what, why, and how. Write your ideas down, read them over.

THE EXERCISE

Imagine you are in a line of traffic driving away from the country at nine o'clock on a Sunday morning in August. This line of traffic is much heavier than you anticipated. Who are these people and why are they leaving the beach instead of going in the opposite direction? Account for the occupants of the six cars in front of you. (For example, the man in the Chevy is going back to town because he just found out his doughnut shop there was broken into at 3:00 A.M. He is pissed.)

THE OBJECTIVE

To train yourself to take off from what you see and hear and create an instant story out of it. To encourage speculation and explore motivation.

STUDENT EXAMPLE

Only a completely macho dude would drive a car like that—a silver Corvette—so it's obvious why he's going back to the city early instead of staying and working on his tan. Clearly, things didn't work out so well with the girl he'd met last night. He'd been hoping that she'd ask him to spend the day with her, but after that shameful performance last night, he just wants to get away as quickly as he can.

Just like the commercial, the family in the wood-paneled station wagon had their money stolen while they were buying flip-flops, and they had to call their weekend short. The boy and girl in the backseat are sucking on McDonald's shakes bought with the little bit of change they found on the car floor, and the husband and wife aren't talking to each other. Each blames the other.

The young woman in the yellow Honda is working the noon-to-five shift today in Filene's men's shirt department and had to leave the party early. She is chewing her nails and hopes she makes it back in time; otherwise, this will be the third time this month she's been late to work.

The old man driving the Oldsmobile is the teenage boy's grandfather. They've just come back from visiting the old man's daughter (the young man's mother) in the insane asylum the day before. They spent the night in a cheap motel. The boy stayed up watching television until 3:00 A.M., while the old man snored. They both couldn't wait to get away from the crazy woman as soon as possible.

The five Chinese people, three men and two women, who are crammed into the K-Car are trying to see as much of the USA as they can in two weeks, before they all have to go back to the University of Utah where they are doing postdoctoral work in the fusion lab. They saw the mountains and then turned around to keep on schedule.

The man and woman in their thirties are lovers and have just spent their first romantic weekend together where they have discovered some things about each other they don't like; he spends too long in the bathroom, she talks about her ex-husband too much. Now they are each feeling a little guilty for lying about having to be back home early.

AMY JENNINGS

117

40

PSYCHO: CREATING TERROR

You like scary? Here's an exercise students have so taken to heart that they report terror-filled, sleepless nights. Many beginning writers shy away from extremes when in fact it's those very tense situations and moments that give fiction its excitement and singularity. You should be able to handle violence, passion, and terror as easily as you do two people having a friendly conversation over a couple of burgers.

THE EXERCISE

You're taking a shower in your house or apartment. You are not expecting anyone and the front door is locked (the bathroom door is not). You hear a strange noise in a room beyond the bathroom. Now, take it from there for no more than two pages. This can be in either the third or the first person. Don't spend any time getting into the shower; you're there when the action begins.

THE OBJECTIVE

To tell a convincing story centered on speculation and terror.

STUDENT EXAMPLE

Ajax, my cat, must have crawled on top of the refrigerator again and knocked over the basket of onions. And now he's playing with the onions—that's the scraping noise—and when I get out of the shower they're going to be all over the floor. Sometimes when Ajax sees another cat he starts to moan and howl, like he's doing now—but he sounds strange. Maybe he's hurt himself.

I pull back the shower curtain and stick my head out to listen. The noise has stopped but I think I just saw something move in the hall. I can't see much from here, but I'm sure a shadow darted past the door. I let the water run over my head again and shut my eyes as the soap runs by, and all of a sudden I feel a draft of cold air. I open my eyes through the soap and hold my breath; the soap stings my eyes. Everything is quiet. All I can hear is the sound of the water, but again I think I see a shadow change. I turn off the water and now I'm breathing fast. I'm standing on the bath mat and Ajax comes in and rubs against my wet legs and then the moaning starts again but it's not the cat, who jumps in fright. I clutch a towel to my chest. I don't know whether to look out into the hall or shut the door. I freeze. Things are crashing in the kitchen, glass breaks; a chair is moved. I slam the bathroom door and manage to lock it even though my fingers are trembling. I'm whimpering. Ajax is hunched in the corner, behind the toilet. The moans grow louder; they're coming closer.

What can I use as a weapon? A disposable razor? A tube of shampoo, a toilet brush, a bottle of Fantastik? I hold this bottle like a gun, my finger on its trigger. I've dropped the towel and I get into the other corner, making small sobbing noises. The moans stop abruptly; then the pounding on the door begins.

HESTER KAPLAN

41

THE NEWSPAPER MUSE:
ANN LANDERS AND
THE NATIONAL ENQUIRER

In her essay, "The Nature of Short Fiction; or, the Nature of My Short Fiction," Joyce Carol Oates says that she is "greatly interested in the newspapers and in Ann Landers' columns and in *True Confessions* and in the anecdotes told under the guise of 'gossip.' Amazing revelations!" She says she has written a great number of stories based on "the barest newspaper accounts ... it is the very skeletal nature of the newspaper, I think, that attracts me to it, the need it inspires in me to give flesh to such neatly and thinly-told tales, to resurrect this event which has already become history and will never be understood unless it is re-lived, re-dramatized."

THE EXERCISE

Collect Ann Landers columns, gossip columns, and stories from *Weekly World News* or *True Confessions* that seem to you to form—either partially or wholly—the basis for a story. Often, these newspaper accounts will be the "end" of the story and you will have to fill in the events leading up to the more dramatic event that made the news that day. Or perhaps the story leads you to ask what is going to happen to that person now.

Clip and save four or five items. Outline a story based on one of them, indicating where the story begins, who the main characters are, what the general tone (that is, the emotional timbre of the work) will be, and from whose point of view you elect to tell the story. These articles can be used for shorter, more focused exercises. For example, describe the car of the person in the article, or the contents of his wallet. Or have the person from the article write three letters.

THE OBJECTIVE

The objective is threefold. One is to look for an article that triggers your imagination and to understand how, when you dramatize the events, the story then becomes *your* story. The second is to increase the beginning writer's awareness of the stories all around us. And third to practice deciding how and where to enter a story and where to leave off.

STUDENT EXAMPLE

One writer used an article from *Weekly World News* about a Japanese moving company that specializes in moving people at "odd times of the day." The service was popular with debtors avoiding creditors and with girlfriends leaving boyfriends. In one case, a woman took her boyfriend to dinner, while the moving company removed her possessions from their apartment.

The Darkness Falls Moving Company

When I went for the job interview, I found the owner in a garage-office, seated at his desk, which wobbled on three legs and a stack of cinder blocks. He was writing in a ledger and stuffing a jelly doughnut into his mouth between calculations.

I cleared my throat and he turned to boom a "Hi there, kid" at me, then wiped his fingers on his shirt and shook my hand. We sat down on the ripped red vinyl of an old car seat and Jake lit up a Marlboro. In between drags, he tried to explain how he'd founded the business, but he kept getting interrupted by calls from potential customers. He'd put each caller on hold, telling them he'd have to check with the personnel department or ask the mechanics about the truck fleet. Then, winking at me, he'd hang the phone over his shoulder and tap his cigarette in the general vicinity of the ashtray, and finally get back on the line to finish the call. When I asked what all that was about, he said he wanted people to think his company was some kind of big deal outfit.

"Impresses the hell out of most of them." He glanced out the door at the company truck—the "fleet" that he'd mentioned on the phone—parked by the curb. "There's another gag I pull. Y'know what people always ask me?" When I shrugged he said, "They ask, 'Where's Darkness Falls?' "

I wanted the job so I humored him. "So what do you say?"

"I tell them it's just south of Northboro. Sometimes I say just east of Westboro. I want them to think that we're a really mysterious outfit."

"What's so mysterious about moving stuff?"

His cigarette ashes fluttered down on my jeans as he leaned toward me. "It's not that simple, Kerry. Let's say you want to be moved with no questions asked, any time of night. Maybe your business wasn't cutting the mustard, so you figure you better move your equipment before the bank moves it out for you. Who do you call? The Darkness Falls Moving Company," he said, grinning. "When you want to make a sudden move, we're the move to make."

Everyone else who interviewed me had given me the look of death when I said I had to quit in September, but Jake just shrugged and said he could use me about four nights a week. "Be prepared to work anytime between dusk and dawn," he said. "I'm the Robin Hood of the moving business."

Scott Weighart

42

THE LETTER HOME

T HE FIRST NOVELS IN THE ENGLISH LANGUAGE WERE IN THE FORM
of letters—so-called epistolary novels, like *Pamela* and *Clarissa*. Few contemporary writers follow their example, but still, use the letter as a fictional device. Tucked into the narrative of a work of fiction, a letter allows the author an especially intimate tone—somewhat like talking into the reader's ear. It's also useful at crucial moments in a plot—in it things get told economically and with a sense of urgency. The Letter Home is a quick and easy way of delivering exposition, characterization, and voice.

THE EXERCISE

You're a senior in college writing home to tell your parent(s) that you're dropping out of school for your last semester; you can't promise that you will ever go back. You want them to understand, if not exactly approve of, your reason(s) for leaving. Make these as specific as you can—and as persuasive. The second half of the exercise is to write the answer, either from one or both of the parents. Limit: 550 words.

THE OBJECTIVE

To get inside the head of another person, someone you have invented, and assume her voice to vary your narrative conveyance.

STUDENT EXAMPLE

Cher Mom and Dad,

I hope you two know how to speak a little French, because I have some news for you that's going to knock your berets right off. Remember I told you that I was taking French this semester? Well, I didn't tell you that my teacher's name was Mademoiselle Pipette and I didn't tell you that I had a crush on her. It turns out that she had a crush on me too, and now we are madly in love. We want to get married because we love each other and so little Pierre or little Gigi will have a dad when he or she arrives at the end of May. I'm going to be a *père!* (That's "father" in French.)

Jeannette can't support us on her teaching salary, so I'm dropping out of college. You've always taught me to be responsible for my actions and this seems like the correct thing to do. I know you'll agree with me on this. I'm going to get a job to support my family and make a home for us. Someday I'll go back to school. I talked to the dean who told me that I have enough credits to reapply later as a second semester freshman.

You two are going to be grandparents! I'm sure you're as excited by all this as I am. College seems unimportant at the moment in the face of these great changes. I know you'll love Jeannette and she sends a *bonjour* to you.

Avec amour (that's "with love"),
Teddy

Dear Teddy,

Forget it. No son of mine is going to drop out of college and get married just because a schoolboy crush on his French teacher went a little too far. I think I know better than you when I say that an eighteen-year-old boy has no conception of what it means to be a responsible father and husband. And what kind of job do you imagine yourself getting? Who's going to hire a boy whose only work experience was mowing his parents' lawn?

I, too, talked to the dean. At the end of the semester, your Mademoiselle Pipette will say good-bye to teaching and to you. I have arranged for her go back to France and have the baby there. I have also gotten her assurance that she and you will have no more contact.

124

I've spared your mother the news of this mindless mess. It would only make her sicker. Though you don't think so now, you will thank me in years to come for getting you out of this situation. In the meantime I suggest you get back to your studies and work hard toward that all-important degree.

Fondly,
Dad

BRIAN FOSTER

Memo from *Atlantic* editors, 1973

Subject: Articles and stories we do not want to read or edit:

Short stories which ask the reader to blame society for misfortunes inflicted on the characters by the author.

43

STRANGER THAN TRUTH

from Rhoda Lerman

THE FICTION WRITER SHOULD BE ABLE TO MAKE ALMOST ANYTHING believable—as Jack Finney does in his masterful novel *Time and Again,* which convinces the reader that it is quite possible to travel backward in time.

THE EXERCISE

A man is having an affair with his secretary. He goes to bed with her in a motel room. When he wakes up in the morning he's in the same motel room but the woman next to him is his wife. Two pages of dialogue. A few lines of action. We can assume description is already in place.

THE OBJECTIVE

A writer needs to be able to imagine an improbable scene and bring it to life. This is a separate issue from making up a story.

STUDENT EXAMPLE

Justin stretched even before he was fully awake. Without opening his eyes he reached over to touch Lily's soft upper arm (she had plenty of flesh on her—just the way he liked his women). But what he felt instead of Lily was unmistakably bony Jane—his wife of eighteen years.

"Janie!"

"Who were you expecting—Missus Santa Claus?"

"You really are at the top of your form, aren't you? The old 8:00 A.M. wit."

Jane turned onto her back. Her Waspy nose pointed at the

ceiling. She said, "Why do we always end up in a dump like this? Look at those stains on the ceiling."

"Did we have a little too much to drink last night?"

"It wouldn't be the first time, lover boy," Jane said. "You finished off about ten beers. *I* was perfectly sober."

"I've got to pee," Justin said. He got up and shut himself in the bathroom. What the hell was going down here? How was it possible to have gone to bed in the Now Voyager Motel with Lily and woken up next to Jane?

His skull felt as if it had crawling things inside it. He splashed cold water on his face and said softly, "Holy shit, I think I must be going crazy." What to do? Maybe if he played it straight the whole thing would right itself, as the world does when you wake from an unsettling dream.

When Justin came out of the bathroom, Jane was sitting up. She was naked. Her breasts looked like they belonged on a fourteen-year-old girl. Why the hell didn't she fatten up like other healthy women?

"Listen, Justin, it was nice of you to suggest we take a holiday from the kids and all, but what exactly did you have in mind?"

"Oh nothing, I just wanted to get away for a night."

Jane nodded, as if she knew something he didn't. "Are you okay, Justin? You look as if you'd just seen a spook?"

"I'm fine," he said. He heard the lie in his own voice.

The thing was, Justin liked his wife's clearheaded style— it was only her body that turned him off. Now his secretary, Lily, she was dumb as dog shit but she was a sensual lass, full of surprises, with lovely fat breasts and a pair of thighs that quivered with joy when he stroked them. It didn't matter that whatever she said sounded stupid.

"Look," he said, "I'm going to take a shower. Do you want to use the bathroom first?"

"That's okay," Jane said. "I want to call home and make sure the kids are getting their breakfast."

Justin went back into the bathroom and turned on the water. Why couldn't the two women simply melt together as one?

CARLA STEIN

127

44

STIRRING UP A FICTION STEW

from Sharon Sheehe Stark

WHEN YOU DON'T HAVE A STORY PUSHING TO BE WRITTEN, IT IS STILL a good idea to write anyway, to exercise language and story. This is especially true for beginning writers who sometimes have to be shown they can "wing it" without knowing exactly where they are going.

THE EXERCISE

Begin a story from random elements such as two characters, a place, two objects, an adjective, and an abstract word. If you are not in a class, give this list to someone and have them provide you with the words so you will be surprised by them. If you are in a class have the class make up a random list. Then everyone must use these elements in the first two pages of a story.

THE OBJECTIVE

To exercise your imagination, to prove to yourself that all you need is a trigger to get you started writing. And if you care about the story you start, the finish will take care of itself.

STUDENT EXAMPLE

Below are the words students chose in a workshop and one student's story written from this list.

pyromaniac	skycap
all-night diner	tuna fish
bowling pin	gardenia
polyester	infinity

Next to the airport: DANTE'S DINER, OPEN 24 HOURS, red neon sign blinking on and off. Red's a cheerful color.

I been night cook here at Dante's for twenty years. Dante, he died last March. House burned down; some pyromaniac lit it. Hell of a thing. Dante's kid owns the place now. Never seen her. But her lawyer came by yesterday—skinny guy, in one of those crummy polyester suits. Asking a lot of questions, sticking his pointy nose into everything. Told me she wanted to sell.

What does she care? So I'm out of a job—so what's it to her? They'll turn the goddamn place into a Lum's or a Hardee's or something. Progress. Premade frozen burgers—premeasured milk shake mix—packaged pie. Progress? Hey, this is a diner: a *diner*, with diner food: hot beef sandwiches, real mashed potatoes, rice pudding, tuna on rye with potato chips and a pickle, and my lemon meringue pie.

I like the people who come in here: skycaps, tourists, kids on dates, hippies, businessmen. Last night a bowling league came in from a tournament over at Airport Lanes. All of them in satin jackets with big bowling pins embroidered on the backs, eating and talking and looking at a couple of pretty girls in the back booth, girls with long hair, shiny pink lips and perfume like gardenias.

I like night work. It's my time. The nights stretch on forever—what's that word? Infinity. The dark outside, all blue, the red neon blinking. Jukebox going. The way I slap my spatula down on the grill, the way I flip eggs over. The way people look when they come in—hungry, tired, and when they leave, they look fed. I get so I'm almost sorry when it's morning. Especially now with that lawyer ruining my day.

GINA LOGAN

VIII: RESOLUTION AND FINAL MEANING

A story is a way to say something that can't be said any other way, and it takes every word in the story to say what the meaning is.
                                        —FLANNERY O'CONNOR

WHEN MEN AND WOMEN BEGAN TELLING TALES AROUND EVENING campfires, surely the most frequent words from their audience were *and then what happens?* Perhaps the only assurance these storytellers had that their story was truly over was someone in the audience saying "tell us another one." It is this last response—"tell us another one" that you want from your readers at the end of your story or novel. If your reader is still saying "And then what happened?" clearly your story isn't over and hasn't achieved the emotional resolution that we talk about in our exercise "It Ain't Over Till It's Over."

Meaning isn't something you start from; it's something you work toward through successive drafts of your story or novel. Flannery O'Connor says it best in her essay "Writing Short Stories" from *Mystery and Manners*. "A story is a complete dramatic action—and in good stories, the characters are shown through the action and the action is controlled through the characters, and the result of this is meaning that derives from the whole presented experience."

Chances are if you start with meaning, if you tell a story to present some general principle, some truth about life, then your story is never going to come alive with specific characters living their specific lives. Meaning is something that emerges as the characters act and react, as the story is written and refined—like the wonderful aroma that arises from the kettle when the ingredients of the stew are present in the right proportions and the cooking time for combining them is just right.

45

TITLES AND KEYS

A TITLE IS THE FIRST THING A READER ENCOUNTERS, AND THE FIRST clue to both initial meaning and final meaning of the story. Look back to the first sentences in the exercise "First Sentences." Notice how many first lines play off the title of the story.

Titles can also be a way of finding stories. Blaise Cendrars once said in an interview, "I first find a title. I generally find pretty good titles, people envy me for them and not only envy me but quite a few writers come to see me to ask for a title."

And until your book is in galleys, you can still change the title. Below are the titles of some famous novels, along with their original titles.

War and Peace—All's Well That Ends Well, by Leo Tolstoy
Lady Chatterley's Lover—Tenderness, by D. H. Lawrence
The Sound and the Fury—Twilight, by William Faulkner
The Great Gatsby—Hurrah for the Red White and Blue, by
    F. Scott Fitzgerald
The Sun Also Rises—Fiesta, by Ernest Hemingway

New York magazine has published a competition for many years. One example is a game in which you were asked to change some famous (and successful) title just enough to make it a loser rather than a winner. The difference between the true ring of the real title and the false note of the parody suggests how good titles are the ultimate test of the exact word, *le mot juste.* Here are some examples.

A Walk on the Wild Side, by Nelson Algren: *A Hike Through Some Dangerous Areas*

One Hundred Years of Solitude, by Gabriel García Márquez: *A Very Long Time Alone*

Girls of Slender Means, by Muriel Spark: *Minimal-Income Young Women*

The Naked and the Dead, by Normal Mailer: *The Nude and the Deceased*

A Farewell to Arms, by Ernest Hemingway: *A Good-bye to War*

The best titles convey some immediate picture or concept to the reader and they do it with an exciting, tantalizing juxtaposition of words.

THE EXERCISE

Have a place in your writer's notebook where you play around with titles, making a list of your favorites. Or read through a story looking for a title to emerge from the story itself—a phrase, an image, etc.

THE OBJECTIVE

To sharpen your instincts for a good title and to understand how titles can lead you to stories.

STUDENT EXAMPLE

Two evocative titles: *Restaurant Thanksgiving*
Company Time

ANNE SPALEK

46

WITH REVISION
COMES FINAL MEANING

It's okay to write the first draft of a story without knowing what the story is about. Flannery O'Connor says, "In fact, it may be better if you don't know what before you begin. You ought to be able to discover something from your stories. It you don't, probably nobody else will." So the discovery should happen during and after a story is written, often during revision.

Stanley Elkin has an effective method for finding out what a story means. He suggests that after five or six drafts, you should write what the story means in one sentence. Then use that sentence to cut, revise, add, adjust, or change the next drafts. Use that sentence as a filter, or a window, to the whole piece.

THE EXERCISE

Write one sentence for a story that is in its fourth or fifth draft. Then revise the story to heighten and illuminate this final meaning.

THE OBJECTIVE

To make you aware of how you come to final meaning slowly, slowly, as you revise a story. To bring you through this process to what you intend the story to mean and what you want to convey to the reader. And finally, to make everything in the story accrue to this final meaning.

47
IT AINT OVER
TILL IT'S OVER

A SHORT STORY AND A SCULPTURE HAVE THIS IN COMMON: NEITHER one existed before its creator imagined and then formed it into the right shape and size. This process includes knowing where to begin and where to end a story, a delicate matter and crucial to whether the story "works" or not. One way to test if your story is truly finished is to anticipate whether your readers are going to ask, "And then what happened?" A complete short story should be like a suspended drop of oil, entire unto itself. Or, viewed another way, it should be psychically "resolved." That is, when the reader gets to the last sentence she will understand that the story stops here—she doesn't have to know what happened to the characters beyond this final moment.

THE EXERCISE

Examine each of your stories carefully to make sure it has this psychic resolution. Read them to a friend or fellow student and ask if they think it's finished. One of the hardest things to learn is how to judge your own work; it's eminently reasonable to try it out on a sympathetic—but objective—listener.

THE OBJECTIVE

To master the art of tying up narrative and thematic threads.

IX: INVENTION AND
TRANSFORMATION

INVENTION AND TRANSFORMATION" COULD HAVE BEEN THE TITLE OF this book. All writing is either inventing something new or a new way to say it, or transforming what is there into how it is there individually for each of us.

But because it isn't the title, we used it as sort of a catchall for some of our exercises that didn't fit into a more specific category such as dialogue—exercises that defied categorization. For example, the last exercise in this part, "Writing Outside the Story," is meant to aid the writer when (1) a story seems stuck or (2) a story is finished but hasn't reached its full potential. These exercises encourage you to write "outside" the story itself—to explore alternatives inherent in your beginnings and to discover possibilities in subsequent drafts.

Another exercise by Lore Segal challenges you to inhabit the mind of your enemy. This exercise underlines something that Rosellen Brown once said. "Fiction always has an obligation to the other side, whatever it is. Finding an adequate angle of vision is the hardest thing about writing it. It's frightening to imagine the inner life of an 'enemy.' But what is more worthwhile?"

The exercise "You Had to Be There" asks you to think of something in the past that wasn't funny when it happened, but now seems to have the makings of a hilarious tale—because of how you tell it. And then there's the exercise on writing compelling sex scenes. (Remember the endless scene in Scott Spencer's *Endless Love* that completely ignored the sense of smell? Didn't believe it, right?)

But enough of this introduction. On to inventing and transforming your own stories.

48

THE INNER LIFE
OF CHARACTERS

WE ALL LEAD INNER LIVES THAT RUN PARALLEL TO WHAT WE ARE actually doing or saying. For example, if you are driving West to start a new job, on the way you might make plans, have fears and hopes, and perhaps feel regrets—all this while traveling at 70 miles per hour on route I-90. The same is true of your characters. They are more than body language and dialogue. Every character has an imagination and you as author must respect this imagination (as distinct from yours) and allow her to use it.

Here are some of the ways your characters will lead their inner lives. With their imaginations they will

hope	fear	wonder	yearn
dread	suspect	project	grieve
plan	judge	plot	envy
lie	repress	pray	relive
regret	dream	fantasize	compose
associate	brood	doubt	feel guilt
speculate	worry	wish	analyze

Philip Roth in *Zuckerman Unbound* has his character Nathan Zuckerman project an entire conversation with his ex-wife/estranged wife, Laura, while on the way to see her. He jumps in a cab and heads for the village with "Time enough, however, for Zuckerman to gauge what he'd be up against with Laura. *I don't want to be beaten over the head with how boring I was for three years.* You weren't boring for three years. *I don't please you anymore, Nathan. It's as simple as that.* Are we talking about sex? Let's then. *There's nothing to say about it ...*" This imagined conversation goes on for several pages until finally Nathan says, "He could only hope that she wouldn't be able to make the case against him as well as he himself could. But knowing her, there wasn't much chance of that." And indeed he has presented her part of the case so well, that Roth doesn't even bring her on stage. Nathan's wife is not home and she never appears in the book, although we feel as if we know her from Nathan's projection of what she might have said to him.

Toni Morrison's Sethe, in *Beloved*, is haunted by the past and laments that her mind just won't stop.

> She shook her head from side to side, resigned to her rebellious brain. Why was there nothing it refused? No misery, no regret, no hateful picture too rotten to accept. Like a greedy child it snatched up everything. Just once, could it say, No thank you. . . . I don't want to know or have to remember that. I have other things to do: worry, for example, about tomorrow, about Denver, about Beloved, about age and sickness not to speak of love.
>
> But her brain was not interested in the future. Loaded with the past and hungry for more, it left her no room to imagine, let alone plan for the next day. . . . Other people went crazy, why couldn't she?

Margaret Atwood's novel *Bodily Harm* ends entirely in the mind of her character Rennie, who says "This is what will happen." She goes on to imagine being saved in passages that alternate with the terrible reality of her situation. Rennie knows there is no real hope—still there is her imagination still hoping in spite of itself.

Alice Hoffman's novel *White Horses* is about a woman who, as a child, was fascinated by her father's tales of Arias. Arias were "men who appeared out of nowhere, who rode white horses across the mesas with no particular destination other than red deserts, the cool waterholes . . ." Men who weren't lost but "never turned back, never went home, they were always traveling west, always moving toward the sun." She runs away with King Connors, a man she thinks is an Aria—even though her father belatedly tells her, "I don't even know if there is such a thing. I may have invented Arias." No matter,

Dina believes in Arias even when her husband turns out not to be one. "When Dina discovered that she was wrong about King, that he was as far from an Aria as a man can be, it was too late, she could never have admitted her error to her father. But these days, Dina felt it had not all been in vain; these days, she was certain her father had been describing someone not yet born." This someone is her son, Silver, whom she descrives as "the perfect stranger she had known forever."

John Irving, in *Hotel New Hampshire*, has John, his narrator, imagine a conversation his parents have with a policeman as they walk past the old Thompson Female Seminary and decide to buy it and turn it into a hotel. The novel is in the first person so John, who is in bed, imagines this scene in the conditional.

> "Wutcha *doin'* here?" old Howard Tuck must have asked them.
>
> And my father, without a doubt, must have said, "Well, Howard, between you and me, we're going to buy this place."
>
> "You *are?*"
>
> "You betcha," Father would have said. "We're going to turn this place into a hotel."

Irving takes us into this scene so convincingly that toward the end he drops the conditional.

> "Wutcha gonna call it?" asked the old cop.
>
> "The Hotel New Hampshire," my father said.
>
> "Holy Cow," said Howard Tuck.
>
> "Holy Cow" might have been a better name for it, but the matter was decided: the Hotel New Hampshire it would be.

After this, we are back with the narrator who says, "I was still awake when Mother and Father came home . . ."

Charles Baxter's story "Gryphon" is told by a young boy fascinated by the wonderful and terrible lessons of his substitute teacher.

> Beethoven, she said, had not been deaf; it was a trick to make himself famous, and it worked. As she talked, Miss Ferenczi's

pigtails swung back and forth. There are trees in the world, she said, that eat meat: their leaves are sticky and close up on bugs like hands. . . . Venus, which most people think is the next closest planet to the sun, is not always closer, and, besides, it is the planet of greatest mystery because of its thick cloud cover. "I know what lies underneath those clouds," Miss Ferenczi said, and waited. After the silence, she said, "Angels. Angels live under those clouds." She said that angels were not invisible to everyone and were in fact smarter than most people. They did not dress in robes as was often claimed but instead wore formal evening clothes, as if they were about to attend a concert.

And finally, the story comes to the point where she casually makes a dire prophecy about one of the narrator's classmates. To witness her imagination at work is an exciting and terrible thing.

The character's imagination is again at work in William Gass's novella "The Pedersen Kid" when the narrator, a teenager, goes down to the crib to see where they found the half-frozen, but still living boy. "Who knows, I thought, the way it's been snowing, we mightn't have found him till spring. . . . I could see myself coming out of the house some morning with the sun high up and strong and the eaves dripping, the snow speckled with drops and the ice on the creek slushing up . . . and I could see myself . . . breaking through the big drift that was always sleeping up against the crib and running a foot right through into him, right into the Pedersen kid curled up, getting soft . . ." Notice how the narrator speculates in concrete, sensory language.

On your own, look for examples of characters using their imaginations: having dreams or nightmares, looking forward to an event with anticipation or apprehension, etc.

THE EXERCISE

Write a story whose forward movement is propelled by:

- a character's belief in something: a tale such as in Alice Hoffman's *White Horses*, a religion, astrology, the *I Ching*, a friend's lie, or winning the lottery
- a character's lie
- a character's suspicions
- a character's guilt
- a character's regrets

Allow something imagined to fire your character's imagination and provide the fuel to cause that character to act and move the story toward some conclusion.

THE OBJECTIVE

To respect the minds and imaginations of your characters. To see how a character's imagination can transcend the confines of a limited point of view—as in *Hotel New Hampshire* and *Zuckerman Unbound*. To allow characters to experience the full range of thought of which we all are capable.

49

SEX IS NOT ALL IT'S CRACKED UP TO BE—IT'S MORE

from Christopher Noël

Anatole Broyard writes that

> sex almost always disappoints me in novels. Everything can be said or done now, and that's what I often find: everything, a feeling of generality or dispersal. But in my experience, true sex is so particular, so peculiar to the person who yearns for it. Only he or she, and no one else, would desire so very much that very person under those circumstances. In fiction, I miss that sense of terrific specificity.

THE EXERCISE

With this caution and exhortation in mind, write a sex scene for a story in which you know your fictional characters well.

THE OBJECTIVE

To gain access to this rich material indirectly so that this universal experience can feel singular, as though coming to be for the first time in history.

STUDENT EXAMPLES

> So this was sex. This is what she had been waiting for. Her eyes began to water from her allergy to the feather pillows his mother had bought him for college. "Don't cry," he said, as if confident that she was overwhelmed by the moment. And when she looked up at him she remembered what had first attracted her: the little bursts of gold in his dangerous gray eyes. She could tell he was worldly, and that he could teach her things.

x

144

On top of her, though, right now, he was no more than dead weight. Twice he poked her in the ribs with his elbow; his feet felt like ice against the tops of her ankles. He could have trimmed his toenails. She bit her bottom lip and tried not to move. She counted the squares of acoustic tile on the ceiling to keep her mind off what he was doing: poking around somewhere between where he was supposed to be and the inside of her right thigh. As soon as she noticed that the roof had once leaked right above their heads—the faded stain the size of an orange was the giveaway—something else occurred to her: he had lied. This was his first time, too.

MARIETTE LIPPO

"Ever feel eggs?" I say, slipping my hand into the bowl, six golden yolks gracefully avoiding my fingers. I catch one up and hold it out to her. She steps back against the stove, but I know it's the reverse of what she meant to do. "See?" I stroke the full, slick globe with one finger of my dry hand, resistance quivering the sac so slightly it could be alive. "If you're careful, they don't break. Feel how perfect," I say, and place her hand atop mine, cupping egg and risking everything in one small motion. For a moment, we don't move; we're seeing, feeling, tasting with our fingers. With the flat, pink palms of our hands. Then she butts a forearm up against my chest and pushes me aside, reaching behind me on the counter for the bowl. Dipping in, she spreads her fingers and pulls up a yolk, a fat one.

"Ever taste eggs?" she says, sliding it inside my mouth before I can resist. The taste is slippery and thick, and my tongue moves without my wanting it. Around the other yolk, the first one, our hands are still together. "Don't break it," she says, laughing, and I hold on, my free hand slipping up beneath her sweater where I find more and more fragile flesh I want to hold, sustain, and burst at the same time. Then she pushes into me like we are dancing, her legs apart, her lips close enough to kiss and I can't stop. The yolk between our tongues, we meet around it, over, under, and I am reaching up between her legs with one desperate, free hand when suddenly she pulls back, thinking twice. Inside my mouth, all yellow goes to liquid and my hopes—so thick—drip sadly down my chin, my throat, hesitating in their viscosity like the tears

145

you hold back, blinking, like everything in the whole world,
chickens, girlfriends, omelet dinners depend on you not
breaking down.

BRIDGET MAZUR

Advice to Young Writers

At one time I thought the most important thing was talent.
I think now that the young man or the young woman must
possess or teach himself, training himself, in infinite patience,
which is to try and to try until it comes right. He must train
himself in ruthless intolerance—that is to throw away anything that is false no matter how much he might love that
page or that paragraph. The most important thing is insight,
that is to be—curiosity—to wonder, to mull, and to muse why
it is that man does what he does, and if you have that, then I
don't think the talent makes much difference, whether you've
got it or not.

WILLIAM FAULKNER, Paris Review interview

50

IT'S ALL IN YOUR HEAD

AVOIDING THE OBVIOUS WHEN WRITING ABOUT EXTREME STATES OF mind is a real challenge for any writer. Resorting to such clinkers as "his heart was in his mouth," "she was on cloud nine," and "he flew off the handle" is far easier than figuring out what is really happening to someone scared, happy, or angry. You must translate the emotion or feeling into fresh, interesting language, rendering precisely or metaphorically what is taking place within the character. Here is Mrs. Dalloway, in Virginia Woolf's novel, experiencing pleasure. "The cook whistled in the kitchen. She heard the click of the typewriter. It was her life, and, bending her head over the hall table, she bowed beneath the influence, felt blessed and purified, saying to herself, as she took the pad with the telephone message on it, how moments like this are buds on the tree of life."

THE EXERCISE

Write three short paragraphs, the first "fear," the second "anger," and the last "pleasure" without using these words. Try to render these emotions by describing physical sensations or images. If you want, write mini-stories, dramatizing these emotions. Try to make your language precise and fresh.

THE OBJECTIVE

To learn to render emotional states without a falling back on tired and imprecise language.

STUDENT EXAMPLE

Fear

Melville found himself abruptly awake and aware of human noises coming from downstairs—the quiet closing of the front door, a step or two in the hallway. His ears rang with concentration as he lay perfectly still. The footsteps came up the stairs, crossed the landing, then moved toward his room. His breath emerged in short, loud gasps. He tried to swallow but his tongue was too dry. The pulse of his heart made loud popping sounds in his ears. Sweat gathered in his armpits. Melville had not moved so much as a finger when he saw the doorknob being slowly turned from the far side of the door. He opened his mouth and attempted to scream but no noise came from his throat. He began to shake violently while his blood slowed within icy veins and arteries.

Anger

A silver Camaro cut in front of Malaver's car, forcing him to slam on the brakes and throwing his body against the steering wheel. At the next light the Camaro was still in front of him; Malaver could see two people sitting so close together they looked as if they were both driving.

"Effing teenagers," Malaver said aloud. "Shouldn't give kids like that licenses." He massaged his neck where it had been hurt and watched sourly as the couple in the Camaro kissed. He tightened his hands on the steering wheel. They kissed again. That's it! He'd had it with these damn kids. He undid his seat belt with trembling fingers, got out of his car and walked up to the driver's side of the Camaro. The girl and boy, wearing twin leather jackets, the girl's yellow hair frizzed as if electrified, returned his stare with clear disdain.

"Bug off, grandpa," the boy said, as the light turned green. The car took flight, burning rubber as it went.

Malaver walked back to his car, got in and began to drive again. All the muscles in his neck and upper body felt as if they were going to rip and shred like wet paper. His head hurt dully. He was sure that if he saw these two again he would do something terrible and violent to them.

Pleasure

Jillie thought the ice cream sundae was beautiful just to look at, and she let it sit in front of her for a minute before starting to eat. The ice cream made her think of being rolled in soft blankets, and the whipped cream was like the clouds outside. The cherry looked like her cat's nose. She took her first spoonful, and as the hot fudge and ice cream made her mouth both hot and cold, she shut her eyes. She curled her toes and moaned. The second bite was even better and she moaned again and giggled. A trickle ran from the corner of her mouth because she was smiling so much. It hung off the side of her chin, and she thought of it as an ice cream tear. She wanted to give everyone she loved a taste, her mother, her father, and her brother, but it was her seventh birthday and she didn't have to share. After another bite, she couldn't control herself any more, and as loud as she could, she screamed, "Oohh, I just love this." When it was all gone, she wiped the inside of the dish with her finger and stuck it in her mouth. She rubbed her stomach and shut her eyes and hummed to herself.

BRIAN FOSTER

51

MY PET

from Alison Lurie

THE FOLLOWING EXERCISE WORKS BEST IF IT IS DONE FIRST AND DIS-
cussed and analyzed afterward.

THE EXERCISE

Write a composition on the subject "My Pet." The only requirement is that this must be a pet you have never owned. It can
be anything from a kitten to a dinosaur, from a fly to a dragon.
Describe what your pet looks like, how you acquired it, what
it eats and where it sleeps, what tricks it can do, and how it
gets on with your family, friends, neighbors, or the people at
work.

NOTES FOR DISCUSSION

We are, we are told, a nation of pet lovers, and more than half
the households in America include an animal, bird, or fish.
What are the motives for keeping a pet? Possible suggestions
are need for protection, need for affection (a creature you can
love and/or one that will love you), aesthetic appreciation (the
beautiful pet as interior decoration), parental feeling (a child
substitute), sadistic impulses (something to maltreat), etc.
What is the function of the pet in your exercise?

A portrait of a pet is also one way of creating a portrait of
its owner. What does this exercise tell us about the pet's owner
(for instance, that he is kind, timid, affectionate, loves beauty,
etc.)?

It has also often been remarked that some people come to
resemble their pets, or vice versa. Why does this happen? In
other cases, the pet is extremely different from the owner; possibly it may express impulses that its owner does not want to

or cannot express (for example, the actively aggressive dog with an apparently passive and peaceful owner). Is the pet in your composition like or unlike its owner, and how?

Animals can play an important part in fiction, and not only in so-called animal stories. Some classic examples are Balzac's "A Passion in the Desert," Kafka's "Metamorphosis," D. H. Lawrence's *The Fox*, and Ursula K. Le Guin's "The Wife's Story." What is the character and function of the pet in your exercise? What is its relation to its owner? How could this description be the basis for a short story?

THE OBJECTIVE

To expand your conception of characters and relationships.

52
FARAWAY PLACES

MANY WRITERS HAVE WRITTEN ABOUT PLACES THEY HAVE NEVER been—Franz Kafka about America in *Amerika*, Saul Bellow about Africa in *Henderson the Rain King*, Thomas Pynchon about postwar Germany in *Gravity's Rainbow*, and Hilding Johnson about India in her story "Victoria"—yet their descriptions of these places persuasively transport the reader there. Below are passages from a novel and a short story.

Finally one morning we found ourselves in the bed of a good-sized river, the Arnewi, and we walked downstream in it, for it was dry. The mud had turned to clay, and the boulders sat like lumps of gold in the dusty glitter. Then we sighted the Arnewi village and saw the circular roofs which rose to a point. I knew they were just thatch and must be brittle, porous, and light; they seemed like feathers, and yet heavy—like heavy feathers. From these coverings smoke went up into the silent radiance.

SAUL BELLOW, *Henderson the Rain King*

Flowers stayed tight in the bud, drying in crisp pods and rattling to the ground one by one in the still night.

The bearers brought half as much water, then still less. The children on the wards slid from whining into torpor.

A sacred cow wandered into the hospital courtyard and could go no further. It was chalky, white, fleshless, its loose dry hide scarred in random constellations, a dessicated wreath of twisted flowers digging into its neck. It stood, eyes closed and head nearly to the ground, for a day and night. Early the next morning I came upon Richard holding a bucket of water beneath the animal's nose.

I said, "We don't have much of that."

"It's what I was allotted for shaving."

I shrugged. "Suit yourself."

In the afternoon the cow knelt, shuddered and died. The sweepers came with great hooks and dragged it out of the courtyard, leaving thin trails of scarlet in the pale dust.

At supper, Richard said, "If they think so much of the beasts, how can they let them suffer?"

"To them they're gods. In general, people don't care much about the suffering of a god. You should know that by now."

HILDING JOHNSON, "Victoria"

THE EXERCISE

Choose a country where you have always longed to go but haven't yet been and set a story there. Read old and new Fodor's guides as well as other recent travel guides and *National Geographic;* buy a map; study the country's politics, religion, government, and social issues; read cookbooks—always, always looking for the persuasive detail, something you would almost have to be there to know.

THE OBJECTIVE

To write with authority and conviction about a place you have never been to.

53

YOU HAD TO BE THERE

Humorous writing is, unfortunately, held in low esteem by the American literary establishment, who believes that if something is funny it can't possibly be serious. This is as false as to deny that people in dire circumstances tell jokes to try to ease the tension or make the situation less intolerable. Beginning writers go along with this, fearing that if they turn out something that makes the reader laugh no one will take them seriously. As a result, almost everything done by the members of writing workshops is sober and earnest. A pity. Anyone who has tried to write humorous fiction knows how extremely difficult it is. Often, a student will substitute archness, euphemism, joke telling, and farce for genuine humor, which should emerge out of character, situation, point of view, and tone. It is not imposed from the outside nor is it verbal embroidery.

The following passage is the beginning of a story by Woody Allen, "The Sacrifice of Isaac." "And Abraham awoke in the middle of the night and said to his only son, Isaac, 'I have had a dream where the voice of the Lord sayeth that I must sacrifice my only son, so put your pants on.' And Isaac trembled and said, 'So what did you say? I mean when He brought this whole thing up.' " If you think this is merely a gag, think twice.

This passage from Evelyn Waugh's novel, *Decline and Fall*, is funny in an entirely different way—relying largely on visual impact rather than on verbal play: "Ten men of revolting appearance were approaching from the drive. They were low of brow, crafty of eye and crooked of limb. They advanced huddled together with the loping tread of wolves, peering about them furtively as they came, as though in constant terror of ambush; they slavered at their mouths, which hung loosely

154

over their receding chins, while each clutched under his ape-like arm a burden of curious and unaccountable shape."

THE EXERCISE

Write about something that happened to you that didn't seem at all funny at the time, for example, being stuck in a traffic jam and having a bee fly in through the car window or the time your tenant set your stove on fire and the firemen wrenched it from the wall and tossed it into the backyard. Bring the incident under the humor spotlight and transform it so as to emphasize things that will make your reader smile or laugh. Pacing is important, as are crucial details, and your own confidence that the story does not need analysis or authorial nudging. The last thing you want to do is tell the reader that you're about to lay a funny story on him. Limit: 550 words.

THE OBJECTIVE

Because humor resides largely in what attitude you assume toward your material, you must be able to discover and exploit those elements that highlight the comic, the exaggerated, and the unlikely. Keep in mind that you could just as easily take the bee story and make it tragic (bee bites driver, driver crashes into another car, killing infant in back seat).

STUDENT EXAMPLE

In the 1970s, boys wore their hair long, over their ears and down the backs of their necks. I was thirteen and my mom and dad used to make me babysit my two younger brothers, Jimmy and Peter. Mom paid me fifty cents an hour. To keep the kids from killing each other, I parked them in front of the TV set until it was time for Peter—who was six that year—to go off to bed. Jimmy was eleven and he hit his little brother every time I turned my back or went to pee or anything.

155

This one night I got an inspiration. "Who wants to make cookies?" I said.

"I do, I do," Peter said.

Jimmy said, "That's girl stuff."

I told him to suit himself and Peter and I went out to the kitchen to round up the ingredients. Peter asked if we could make chocolate chip cookies and I said sure we could. I got out the stuff we needed and plugged in the Mixmaster Dad got Mom for Christmas. Pete dragged a chair over to the counter and stood on it so he could see what was going on.

Pretty soon Jimmy joined us and even asked if he could help. Pete said no but I said yes and since I was the boss what I said went. We measured out the flour, and poured in all the chips in the bag, and then the other things and dumped the dough into the electric mixing bowl. "Okay," I told Peter. "Ignition."

He pushed the button and the blades began to move through the dough. When I went to check on the oven, Peter must have leaned way over because the next thing I heard was him screaming bloody murder. "Help, hey, it's got my hair, hey turn it off!"

I gaped: Peter's head was practically inside the bowl and one long lock of his hair was being twisted around the knob holding the blades, pulling him closer and closer to the blades. Just like James Bond.

Jimmy shrieked, "Yikes! It's eating Peter. The mixer's eating Peter!"

But was he doing anything about it? No way. I rushed over and turned it off. Peter wrenched his head away, fell off the chair, and landed on the floor, holding his head and screaming bloody murder. For some reason, there was no blood but he had a bald spot the size of a large mixing spoon.

We had to throw away the cookie dough—it was full of Peter's hair. He wore his Red Sox cap day and night for the next three weeks. Mom never figured out why.

TERRY FRENCH

54

THE ENEMY'S LIFE

from Lore Segal

Y OUR FIRST JOB AS A WRITER OF STORY IS TO MAKE UP THE PEOPLE to whom your story will happen. Not one character, but several, many, all of whom live inside their own bodies, look out of their own eyes at a different world.

THE EXERCISE

Week one
Write a scene that brings to fictional life someone you hate. Make the reader hate her. It might be someone who annoys you—someone whose manner you can't stand, whose voice grates on you. Or it might be someone who has offended you or done you some harm, or someone to whom you have done some harm—there are many reasons to hate people. If you have the courage, take on someone who is evil on the grand scale. It can be someone you know, someone you know about, or, best of all, invent a real nasty.

Week two
Write the same scene, from the point of view of the nasty, and write it in the first person.

THE OBJECTIVE

Story and only story is the peaceable kingdom where you and I and the next fellow can lie down on the same page with one another, not by wiping our differences out, but by creating our differences on the page. Only on the page of a story can I look out of your and my and the other fellow's eyes all at the same time.

157

STUDENT EXAMPLE

Week one

"Doctor" Andrews, as he styled himself, was one of those white men who can be taken seriously no place in the world except an obscure bush country in Africa. He was a Canadian health program administrator, trained as a nurse, with a minimal knowledge of medicine, yet blessed with a kind of bureaucratic power in the Republic of Songhai by virtue of his control over the medical aid program provided by a generous Canadian government. He was a plump, rosy, voluble, man with tiny white teeth in an insincere smile.

I met him when he arrived one day to inspect my clinic. He bustled around, looked over the shoulder of one of my Mandinka aides who was sewing up a gash in a boy's leg and said superciliously, "Not very sterile, you know. But I suppose they've never heard of the concept." I mentioned that we did use antiseptics, kept the surgery room as clean as possible, and did scrub before even minor procedures, but he paid no attention.

He inspected my three shelves of medicines and sniffed. "What do you call this?" he asked.

I took the opportunity to put in my oft-frustrated request. "We have lots of infections here," I said, "and one of the things we could use is a supply of penicillin. I know the Canadian program has a steady supply and I wonder if you could spare me some from time to time?"

He turned and looked at me as if I had demanded his wallet. "Really!" he said. "You do have grandiose ideas about practicing in the bush. I think you should realize that we need every gram of medication we have for the government hospital in the city. For the kind of patient who counts."

Week two

The first day I met him in a remote Mandinka village, he was asking for penicillin. The American hadn't even been here a month yet, and already he thought he could set our whole health care system on its head and shake miracles out of its pockets. I knew he would blunder ahead and upset the Africans with his persistent demands; Peace Corps is full of self-important American youngsters who little realize the damage they're capable of inflicting on fragile, carefully constructed

158

development projects like ours—initiated a decade before anyone even thought of inviting the USA in.

The Canadians make a point of sending qualified people here, and of briefing us meticulously. But the American knew little about the health care system over which he raged; he couldn't see the impossibility and the dangers of shipping penicillin out to a bush clinic where the natives had never even see a Band-Aid; he thought that just because he had arrived, we would scramble to meet his every need—he had no notion of how hopelessly overworked we are, and will be for many years to come, in the involved process of establishing this system. If Peace Corps had courteously offered his services to us in advance, instead of flinging him pointlessly out into the bush, he could have become a useful member of our team. Now he's no more than a gadfly—another obstacle to be worked out. It wouldn't take much to get him transferred— or better yet, deported.

I still wonder why we didn't go ahead and get rid of him.

CAMERON MACAULEY

55

TAKING RISKS

ONE OF THE GREAT PLEASURES OF WRITING FICTION IS LETTING YOUR imagination and fantasies take off anywhere they want to go. Most people feel guilty when they think of doing something awful to someone they dislike; writers can invent a story and in it fling a hated character from a moving car or have him go blind. Another fantasy you can play out is doing something the very idea of which terrifies you—like parachuting from a plane or sailing across the ocean solo. As a fiction writer you're at a serious disadvantage if you can't write about an experience you're unlikely ever to know firsthand. This is not as easy as it seems, because you must sound not only plausible diving to the depths of the Aegean, you've also got to know what you're talking about—all those details about the scuba gear have to sound absolutely authentic. This is why a lot of novelists spend so much time in libraries—they're making sure they get it right.

THE EXERCISE

Using the first person, describe an event or action you are fairly sure you will never experience firsthand. Be very specific—the more details you incorporate the more likely it is that your reader will believe you. Include your feelings and reactions. Limit: 550 words.

THE OBJECTIVE

"Write what you know" is all very well but it certainly does restrict most of us within narrow confines. You must also be able to write what you don't know, but can imagine. This is what your imagination is for. Let it fly.

160

56

TOTAL RECALL

from Alison Lurie

THE FOLLOWING EXERCISE WORKS BEST IF IT IS DONE FIRST AND DIS-
cussed and analyzed afterward.

THE EXERCISE

*This exercise should be done with two or more people; one to
read the instructions aloud while the others concentrate on re-
calling the experience. Read slowly and pause between sentences and paragraphs; the whole process should take at least
five minutes.*

Shut your eyes. Go back in your mind to some summer or
part-time job you had in the past. Look at the surroundings in
which you were working. See the place in which you worked:
factory, schoolroom, restaurant, hospital, store, library, whatever. Or perhaps it is an outdoor scene: beach, road, garden,
construction project, ranch, café. Notice the shapes and colors
of what is around you. Look at the materials with which you
are working, note their shapes and colors.

Now look at the other people who are present in this scene:
coworkers, boss, customers in the restaurant or shop, children
at camp, or a babysitting job. Choose one person and observe
her closely; notice what she is wearing and the expression on
her face. What is she doing as you watch? What gestures is
she making?

Now begin to hear the sounds that belong to this scene.
The clank of machinery, the sizzle of hamburgers cooking on the
grill, the splash of water in the pool, the ringing of phones,
the thump and hum of music, whatever it may be. Listen to
the voices: what are they saying? Perhaps you will hear a line
or two of dialogue. What is the person you especially observed
saying, and what do you or someone else say in reply?

Now allow yourself to experience the smells that belong to this scene: food cooking, fresh-cut grass, motor oil, sweat, flowers, disinfectant, whatever. If you are working in a restaurant or bar, or eating on the job, you may want to become aware of taste too: the lukewarm bitterness of instant coffee in a plastic cup, the sugary chocolate slickness of a candy bar hidden in your desk drawer.

Look around you at this point and become aware of the climate of your surroundings. Is it winter or summer? If you are working outdoors, what is the weather like? What time of day is it? If you are indoors, is the air stuffy or fresh, smoky or clear? What can you see out the window?

Next, become aware of the sense of touch, of the textures of the things you are working with: soft or rough, smooth or fuzzy, wet or dry. Notice heat and cold: the damp, icy feel of a glass of soda, the warm silky texture of a child's hair; the hot oily parts of a broken lawnmower.

Now turn your sense of touch inward; become aware of the motions you are making and the sensations in your muscles: the strain of lifting sacks of dirt or cement, the pleasure of stirring cake batter round a big stainless-steel bowl, the weight of a tray of drinks on your shoulder.

Finally, notice your emotions. Do you like this job or hate it? Are you interested in what is going on around you or bored? Are you tired and depressed or in good spirits? Where will you go when work is over for today?

Do you like or dislike the people around you? What do you feel about the person you chose to observe? What do you think she feels about you? What would you like to say to her? If you said it, what would this person probably say or do?

When all these things are clear in your mind, but not until then, open your eyes and record them as rapidly as possible. Write in the present tense. Don't bother about legible hand-writing, complete sentences, or spelling words correctly: the point is to get this material down on paper while it is still fresh and vivid in your memory. You are not composing a story, only making notes.

NOTES FOR DISCUSSION

Writers differ in their sensitivity to the world. Some especially notice shapes, some smells, some colors, some textures; some see gestures, others see clothes or facial expressions. James Joyce, whose eyesight was poor, perceived the world mainly in terms of words and sounds; Thomas Wolfe, a large man with an even larger appetite, was famous for his awareness of the tastes and odors of food.

As you look over your notes, ask yourself whether there are kinds of perception you are neglecting in your writing, or passing over too rapidly. Do you habitually describe scenes and people in black and white, for instance? If you are doing this exercise in a group, read your notes aloud and ask the other people present what they noticed about your strengths and weaknesses of recall. Once you are aware that you don't always remember to include colors, smells, sounds, texture, or whatever, you can make a conscious effort to do so, and your writing will become more vivid.

If this exercise worked especially well for you, perhaps it could be turned into a story. Suppose the two main characters were you and the person you observed and spoke to, what might happen between them? What change in them or in their relationship might take place?

No matter what you are writing, you can use this technique. If you like, you can concentrate on people rather than scenes; visualize them in detail, see what they are doing, hear their words, etc. Once you become really familiar with the process, it is not even necessary to go back in imagination to a real scene or a real person; you can call up an invented character or event in the same way.

THE OBJECTIVE

To make some experience as vivid as possible, to recall it in full sensual and emotional detail before you begin to write.

57

WRITING OUTSIDE THE STORY

from Elizabeth Libbey

Sometimes a story feels as if it hasn't reached its full potential. You know it isn't finished yet, but you are not sure how to proceed in revising it. Another draft doesn't seem to be the answer, nor do you want to put it aside for a while. This is the time when "writing outside" the story might be the way to return to working inside it.

There are different ways to write outside a story. Some of the methods have to do with exploring the inner life of your main character through diary entries, letters to other characters, dreams, or lists. Or you might try writing a missing scene or a scene that occurred before the beginning of the story. Or perhaps you avoided a confrontation scene or stopped your story too soon. Even if you don't use this material in the story, it will, as Hemingway said, make itself felt.

THE EXERCISE

Pull out one of your stories that doesn't feel finished. Have your main character do the following exercises—as if he had his own notebook. For example, maybe you write with a number 2 pencil, but your character prefers to use a Rapidograph pen. Go with the pen. Remember, your character is doing this exercise—not you, the author!

So, as your main character:

- make a diary entry for the time of the story
- make a diary entry for the time preceding the story
- write a letter to someone not in the story about what is happening in the story
- write a letter to someone in the story

Or you might explore places in the story that you haven't either dramatized or summarized. Examples:

■ Have your characters avoided a confrontation? (This is a natural reaction—we are all nonconfrontational and, therefore, we often allow our character to avoid the very scenes and confrontations that we would avoid.) Does your story have missing scenes?

■ What events happened before the beginning of the story? Before page one? Try writing scenes of those events that most affected the beginning of the story. Maybe you started the story later than you should have.

■ Write past the ending. Maybe your story isn't really finished. Perhaps you are avoiding the confrontation scene because you aren't really sure what your characters would say to each other.

THE OBJECTIVE

To explore aspects of a story that may seem, at first, to be on the periphery, but at closer look can deepen or open it up. Nothing is ever lost by more fully knowing the individual world of each story. And it's better to let your characters speak for themselves.

X: MECHANICS

As we wrote in the introduction, to produce good fiction you have to *think* like a writer (be open, skeptical, curious, forgiving, and passionate). The other, equally important, requirement is to master the techniques of the craft (and, not incidentally, get rid of bad habits).

What we call "mechanics" includes simple matters such as when—and especially when not—to use adjectives and adverbs, how to recognize and avoid word packages, and how to vary the sound of your sentences. Then there are more subtle techniques, like keeping a story alive and making sure that your story has the right pace and proportions.

A few fortunate people who have never written anything seem to be able to sit down and write and make it sing; most of us, however, have to go through a long apprenticeship of trial, error, and often tears. First drafts are apt to be a mess—this holds true for even the most accomplished writers. The techniques you use over and over again—being as ruthless as the toughest editor—should take you from mess to controlled and, quite possibly, exciting works of fiction.

58

IDENTIFYING STORY SCENES
DURING REVISION

WHEN A STORY ISN'T WORKING, IT OFTEN HELPS TO LOOK AT IT IN A new way—not just in hard-copy manuscript or on your computer screen—but with scissors and tape and a conference table.

In her book *The Writing Life*, Annie Dillard says she has often "written" with the "mechanical aid of a twenty-foot conference table. You lay your pages along the table's edge and pace out your work. You walk along the rows; you weed bits, move bits, and dig out bits, bent over the rows with full hands like a gardener." Thus one method for revising, or "reenvisioning" a story, is to become very self-conscious about its shape when it is laid out in front of you in pieces.

THE EXERCISE

Choose a story that doesn't seem to be working and cut it apart into the separate components of scenes and narrative passages. Lay these story pieces out on a large table and just take in what is in front of you. How many scenes do you have? Are there too few or too many? Are there any "missing" scenes? What would happen if you rearranged the sequence of events? What would happen if you begin with the beginning of the ending scene and use it to frame the story?

THE OBJECTIVE

To see an early draft of a story as something that isn't etched in stone. Not only are the words and lines capable of being revised, but the story structure itself is often still fluid enough to rearrange and analyze for the questions listed above.

STUDENT EXAMPLE

One student had a twelve-page story that wasn't working, and when she cut the story apart, was astonished to discover that although it was a short story, it had seventeen separate scenes. She eliminated eight of those scenes by summarizing or omitting them altogether and ended up with a publishable story.

Writing is a hard way to make a living, but a good way to make a life.

DORIS BETTS

59

DYNAMIC SCENING

from Thalia Selz

The playwright Harold Pinter writes about creating drama from the "battle for positions." He pointed out that threat—and thus the necessary tension—arises from having people in a confined space battling over dominance and over "what tools they would use to achieve dominance and how they would try to undermine the other person's dominance." Pinter's scene dynamics work not only for plays but equally well for scenes in short fiction and novels.

THE EXERCISE

Examine a scene you are having trouble with, one that (1) demands action, although not necessarily physical action, and (2) provides a turning point in your story. If you don't yet have such a scene in your story, try writing one. Make it at least three pages long, although five pages will give you a greater chance to develop the personal dynamics and show how the balance of power can keep changing. Tish, discovering that Mort has cheated her in a business deal, confronts him with evidence that would stand up in court, forcing him to return funds he has stolen. Alycia, a charming jewel thief, is caught in the act by her intended victim—an attractive diamond merchant—and seduces him, ensuring both his silence and the gift of a handsomely insured necklace.

THE OBJECTIVE

To show that by the time the scene is over the position of dominance has changed while the characters remain consistent and credible throughout.

60

HANDLING THE PROBLEMS OF TIME AND PACE

from Robie Macauley

THE TRADITIONAL RULE IS THAT EPISODES MEANT TO SHOW IMPORTANT behavior in the characters, to make events dramatic as in theater, or to bring news that changes the situation should be dealt with in the scenic, or eyewitness manner. Stretches of time or occurrences that are secondary to the story's development are handled by means of what is called a narrative bridge. Dialogue is the direct report of speech; indirect discourse is the summary of what was said. Some examples follow.

Scenic

Now they were at the ford, the rain was still falling, and the river was in flood. John got out of the jeep and stared at the white violence of the water they must cross to reach the place where the muddy road picked up again.

Narrative summary

The journey to Punta Gorda took two days by near-impossible road. At one point, they had to cross a raging river and follow a muddy track that only a jeep could manage.

Dialogue

"Now how are we going to get across this monster?" Lisa asked.

"Easy," said John. "We take the rope over, get it around that big tree and use the winch to pull the jeep across."

"But who swims the flood with the rope?"

"Well, I can't swim," he said, "but you're supposed to be so good at it."

Indirect discourse

When they came to the swollen river, John suggested that they put a rope across and then use the jeep's winch to pull

172

the vehicle to the farther bank. Because Lisa had talked so often about her swimming ability, he suggested ironically that she be the one to take the rope over.

THE EXERCISE

Here are the events that might make a long short story. Write a scenario in which you indicate

■ Where you would place a full scene or incidental scene.
■ Where you would use summaries, either narrative summaries or summarized scenes and indirect discourse.

In her final year in medical school in the 1970s, Ellen fell in love with a young intern at the teaching hospital. His name was Gamal and he came from Lebanon. Although Gamal was not political himself, his younger brothers were involved in radical Arab politics.

Ellen's New England Jewish family had always been liberal. Her father, Mark, was a lawyer who had defended Black Panthers in the 1960s and antiwar activists in the 1970s. Her mother, Sarah, a writer, was equally liberal. They were both fervently pro-Israel.

When Ellen brought Gamal home for the winter holidays, the situation grew very tense as one by one, Israel, religion, politics, and child-rearing practices seemed to crop up in their conversations. Although Ellen was uncomfortable at times, she felt that love was more important than politics.

Mark and Sarah were meticulously polite and tolerant in Gamal's company, but they worried in private. They'd always supported Ellen's decisions, but now, they thought, she was about to ruin her life.

The wedding was set for June at the parents' house in Connecticut. It would be a small affair because relatives on both sides would refuse to come. But Mark and Sarah rationalized a lot and put the very best face on it.

The day came. Everything was ready. There was going to be a civil ceremony—a compromise—and then a garden party at Ellen's home.

When Mark got up that morning, he turned on the television news. The lead story was about the bombing and destruction of a TWA plane in Greece by terrorists. Gamal's two brothers had been arrested as prime suspects. Mark and Sarah confronted Ellen and Gamal.

Now you resolve the story.

THE OBJECTIVE

To learn to identify which parts of a story should be presented in a scene and which parts of a story should be summarized. To develop an understanding of pace.

61
THE POWER OF "SEEMED" AND "PROBABLY"

Beginning writers often think that they have to go into the heads of all their characters in order for the reader to know what they are thinking. They forget that people can reveal themselves in a myriad of ways: dialogue, body language, and so forth. They also forget that in reality no one has access to another person's thoughts and that, in addition to listening to what those close to us say and observing how they act, we are constantly assuming, suspecting, projecting, and imagining what they think.

Learn to give your characters (especially the point-of-view character) the same imagination that you have. An example of this occurs in a Bartholomew Gill mystery novel, *McGarr and the Politician's Wife*. The entire plot turns on the word *seemed*. A man, Ovens, has a head injury and is lying in a coma. The detective goes to see him and needs to know if he might have just fallen or if there was foul play. He asks the doctor if Ovens can speak and the doctor says not for another forty-eight hours.

The author writes, "Ovens' eyes, however, seemed to contradict the assessment of the insouciant young doctor. Dark brown, almost black, they told McGarr that Ovens knew the score: that his was not merely a medical problem that a favorable prognosis could eliminate, that whoever had done this to him had a very good reason, and those eyes, suddenly seeming very old, realized his troubles weren't over." So McGarr doesn't have to wait forty-eight hours. He starts his investigation immediately.

Ann Beattie's use of the word *probably* in her story "Afloat" indicates that the story is not third person from the point of view of the sixteen-year-old child who is introduced at the beginning of the story. Beattie writes, "When she was a little girl she would stand on the metal table pushed to the front of the deck and read the letters aloud to her father. If he sat, she sat. Later, she read them over his shoulder. Now she is sixteen, and she gives him the letter and stares at the trees or the water or the boat bobbing at the end of the dock. It has probably never occurred to her that she does not have to be there when he reads them." Sentences later, after the letter is presented, the first-person narrator comes in with "He hands the letter to me, and then pours club soda and Chablis into a tall glass for Annie and fills his own glass with wine alone."

THE EXERCISE

Write a scene involving two characters. Have the point-of-view character presume something entirely different about the situation from what the other character's overt behavior seems to imply. For example, a landlord comes to visit, and the tenant suspects that it isn't a visit but an inspection. Make up several situations in which one character can fantasize or project or suspect or even fear what another character is thinking.

THE OBJECTIVE

To show how your characters can use their imaginations to interpret the behavior and dialogue of other characters.

62

BRINGING ABSTRACT
IDEAS TO LIFE

ONE OF THE PRINCIPAL PROBLEMS IN WRITING STORIES IS TO MAKE abstract ideas come to life. It is not enough to talk of poverty or ambition or evil, you must render these ideas in a concrete way with descriptive sensory details, similes, and metaphors. Examine how growing old is handled in Muriel Sparks's *Memento Mori*, poverty in Charles Dickens's *Bleak House* and Carolyn Chute's *The Beans of Egypt Maine*, racism in Ralph Ellison's *Invisible Man*, growing up in Frank Conroy's *Stop-Time*, ambition in Theodore Dreiser's *An American Tragedy*, and evil in William Golding's *Lord of the Flies*.

THE EXERCISE

Make several of the following abstractions come to life by rendering them in concrete specific details or images.

racism	poverty
injustice	growing up
ambition	sexual deceit
growing old	wealth
salvation	evil

THE OBJECTIVE

To learn to think, always, in concrete terms. To realize that the concrete is more persuasive than any high-flown rhetoric full of fancy words and abstractions.

STUDENT EXAMPLES

Racism
not sitting next to a minority person on the subway
SANFORD GOLDEN

referring to others as "you people"
FRED PELKA

Poverty
checking for change in the telephone booth
SANFORD GOLDEN

a young boy carrying water to an abandoned building where his family is living.
MOLLY LANZAROTTA

Sexual deceit
splashing on Brut to cover the smell of a woman's perfume
SANFORD GOLDEN

keeping a pair of clean underwear in your pocketbook
SUSAN HIGGINS

Growing old
not making it across street before light flashes "Don't Walk."
SANFORD GOLDEN

the stairs become a place of treachery
JIM MEZZANOTTE

Evil
"Let's sell tickets to the rape."
FRED PELKA

purposely running down animals on the road
SANDY YANNONE

Prejudice
Victoria slipped the camphor between her skin and her undershirt before opening the library door. Her mother made her wear it from Rosh Hashanah to Passover, a guard against winter colds, "In Poland it was colder," she always said, "yet we never got sick in the winter." It was useless for Victoria

178

to point out that one aunt and uncle had died in Polish winters despite their health charms.

She placed her bag of books on the library's high stone counter where "Returns" was written in a beautiful penmanship. "I hope you didn't tear any of these," Mrs. Holmes said, pausing in her friendly chat with a woman who looked like Betty Crocker. One by one she checked in the ragged copies of kids' classics saying that sometimes it looked as if Victoria had eaten her dinner on these books. She smiled to the woman. "Everything turns into rags in their hands, you know."

Victoria went to sit in the children's section of the library. Three new books were displayed on the table. She might get through by closing time. She knew Mrs. Holmes wouldn't let her take out these books till yellow tape obscured some of the words. She wondered if it might make a difference if Mrs. Holmes knew that she was the best reader in the whole fifth grade.

BARBARA SOFER

63

THE FIVE-HIGHLIGHTER EXERCISE

from David Ray

GOOD WRITERS MUST, OF COURSE, BE GOOD READERS, AWARE OF TEXture and the orchestration of sense impressions that make vivid fiction. Really powerful writing is memorable for visual sweep or for tactile detail, for near-palpable sensations of touch or near-audible music. Memories of taste are cited when readers speak of Proust. Indeed, great fiction has the power of poetry. A E. Housman described that power as recognizable "by the symptoms which it provokes in us . . . when I am shaving . . . if a line of poetry strays into my memory, my skin bristles so that the razor ceases to act." We need to evoke this power to move readers physically.

A look at the begining of Stephen Crane's "The Open Boat," for example, reveals a vivid passage dominated by visual imagery. Alice Munro's "How I Met My Husband" starts with auditory and kinetic energy, followed by a dash of color and a scream: "We heard the plane come over at noon, roaring through the radio news, and we were sure it was going to hit the house, so we all ran out into the yard. We saw it come in over the treetops, all red and silver, the first close-up plane I ever saw. Mrs. Peebles screamed." The following passage from Nelson Algren's *The Man with the Golden Arm* is typical of that writer's command of a full palette:

> This time she was protected against the light, standing in her fresh white dress and the little blood-red earrings against the sallow olive of her cheeks and the midnight darkness of her hair. The hair that swept down over her shoulders as if touched by the wind that drove the curtains aside when the long Els stormed overhead. She was looking less careworn since John had left her.
>
> "I just thought you'd like to see a dog that drinks beer,"

Frankie apologized, "you told me to get one of my own to kick."

"I didn't say nothin' about a beer-drinkin' one, Frankie," she protested as gravely as a child. "But if you want we'll try him out." Rumdum, at first listening only listlessly, picked up suddenly and hauled Frankie forward into the room.

"The smell of Budweiser makes him powerful," Frankie explained. Before she could get the saucer filled Rumdum had licked the saucer dry and Frankie had to clamp his snout with both hands, the great hound whimpering brokenheartedly, till she could get it filled again without losing a finger.

"He ain't had a drink all day." Frankie sympathized with all dry throats. "Fact is, I ain't neither." He pulled the bottle off his hip with feigned surprise at finding it there. "Look what some guy stuck in my pocket!"

"I'll stick to beer," Molly told him cautiously. "I been on the wagon since John's gone." She turned to the little combination record player on the dresser while he drank.

"Everythin' is movin' too fast," the record complained drowsily.

THE EXERCISE

Using five different-colored highlighters, mark a text with a different color for each sense impression, e.g., blue for visual, red for auditory, green for taste, etc. Synaesthesia would, of course, be indicated by more than one color. Writers vary greatly in terms of the dominance of one sense or another. The goal, though, is to find passages using all five senses—then to write such passages.

THE OBJECTIVE

To heighten awareness of the need for a full repertory of sense evocations in good writing. Ideally you should call forth all five senses as well as synaesthesia. The writer thereby evokes from the reader a full range of responses.

64

SUIT YOUR SENTENCE
TO ITS MEANING

from Thalia Selz

MANY STORIES ARE UNCONVINCING BECAUSE THE WRITER IS USING the wrong kinds of sentences for the material and mood. A string of short subject-verb-object sentences can sound infantile instead of sounding excited like the Robert Boswell passage below. Or a stream-of-consciousness passage may merely list scattered details instead of using them to create scene and mood like the montage by Dos Passos.

"All fiction has style," says Stephen Minot in *Three Genres*. "But it is important to examine just what your style is and then to judge whether it is the best possible approach for a particular story." Both Minot and John Gardner, in *The Art of Fiction*, carefully examine the sentence as an element of style, and their observations can help any writer.

THE EXERCISE

Read the following passages to see how the writers convey information while shaping our attitudes and emotions.

In Ernest Hemingway's *The Sun Also Rises* an obscure character is killed by a bull being taken to the bullring in a Spanish town. The first brief sentences deliver the objective facts almost as coolly as a newspaper obit. The final two sentences are longer and have a more complex structure (why?), and the string of ten short prepositional phrases that ends the passage not only mimics the rhythm of the train wheels but creates a poetic, lulling, hypnotic effect, suggestive of a chant.

> Later in the day we learned that the man who was killed was named Vicente Girones, and came from near Tafalla. The next day in the paper we read that he was 28 years old, and had a farm, a wife, and two children.... The coffin was loaded into

182

the baggage-car of the train, and the widow and the two children rode, sitting, all three together, in an open third-class railway-carriage. The train started with a jerk, and then ran smoothly, going down grade around the edge of the plateau and out into the fields of grain that blew in the wind on the plain on the way to Tafalla.

In *The Big Money*, John Dos Passos describes Rudolph Valentino's progress through a city.

the streets were jumbled with hysterical faces, waving hands, crazy eyes; they stuck out their autographbooks, yanked his buttons off, cut a tail off his admirably tailored dress suit . . . his valets removed young women from under his bed; all night in nightclubs and cabarets actresses leching for stardom made sheepseyes at him from under their mascaraed lashes.

Cynthia Ozick's short story "The Shawl" takes place in a concentration camp during World War II. The child Magda is so attached to her shawl that she can be hidden away from the guards inside it.

She tangled herself up in it and sucked on one of the corners when she wanted to be very still.
    Then Stella took the shawl away and made Magda die.
    Afterward Stella said: "I was cold."
    And afterward she was always cold, always. The cold went into her heart . . .

And from Robert Boswell's "The Darkness of Love":

She stood. They held each other, afraid to talk. Louise led him out of the living room into the hall. She opened the door to the walk-in closet and spread the comforter.

Now rewrite a passage of your own trying to make the words, the length of the sentences, and their syntactical rhythms express as nearly as possible both the information you want to convey and the attitudes and emotions you want your reader to feel.

THE OBJECTIVE

To shape sentences to do your bidding. Sentences aren't just snowshoes to get you from the beginning to the end of your story. They are powerful tools with which to carve a story that wasn't there until you decided to create it.

STUDENT EXAMPLES

Notice how these students combine sentence length and rhythm with meaning.

"It's tonight."
"Who?"
"Hoffman."
"How?"
"We suicide him. Booze and pills."

BOB PELTIER

Jeannie's hands drew Ferris-wheel circles in the air, turning an invisible car back over front, front over back, the invisible car larger than the metal Matchbox cars Tim had played with as a child and smaller, smaller, smaller than the silver Honda in which he had died.

TERY GRIFFIN, "Holding On"

You're wasting time sitting in a doctor's office when you could be traveling or meeting famous people. Really sick kids always get to meet famous people. But you know you aren't dying because you feel and look fine. How can anything serious be wrong if you look fine?

GAIL FEINBERG, "A Coming of Age Story"

I held the seat of the bicycle, aiming it into the alley, and headed down the grayness toward home.

DOUG LLOYD, "Fewer Happy Endings"

65
WORD PACKAGES
ARE NOT GIFTS

A WORD PACKAGE IS A GROUP OF NEUTRAL WORDS STRUNG TOGETHER into a hackneyed phrase. Word packages are used by lazy writers searching for an easy way out of a difficult or slippery thought. (Frequently they are found at the beginnings of sentences.)

THE EXERCISE

Stay away from the following word packages. They signal to the smart reader that you lack freshness and are an uninteresting writer.

Better than ever
For some curious reason
A number of . . .
As everybody knows
She didn't know where she was
Things were getting out of hand
It came as no surprise
It was beyond him
Needless to say
Without thinking
He lived in the moment
Well in advance
An emotional roller coaster
Little did I know

THE OBJECTIVE

To purge yourself forever of stale and/or imprecise language.

66

SPICE: VARYING
SENTENCE STRUCTURE

JOHN UPDIKE SAYS THAT THE BEST WAY TO GET THE KINKS OUT OF your prose is to read it aloud. Reading aloud what you have written reveals its flaws in the same way a magnifying glass reveals blemishes on your skin.

Keep in mind that the eye and ear are connected and that what the reader sees will somehow be transmitted to his inner ear. Too many sentences with a similar construction will make your reader yawn. You should always read your work aloud before showing it to anyone. Doing this will help you avoid monotony, repetition, flatness, unintentional alliteration, and other impediments to smooth, fluid prose.

The following passage from Mavis Gallant's story, "The Four Seasons" is an example of prose that sings when read both silently and aloud. "The sea was greener than anything except Mrs. Unwin's emerald, bluer than her sapphire, more transparent than blue, white, transparent glass. Wading with a twin in each hand, she saw their six feet underwater like sea creatures. The sun became white as a stone; something stung in its heat, like fine, hard, invisible rain."

THE EXERCISE

Write a description in which the sentences are variously built. The subject should not always be the first word; some sentences should be longer than others. Read aloud the work of an author you admire and see how he or she accomplishes this. It's all right to imitate.

THE OBJECTIVE

Prose is both utilitarian and decorative. Unless you're deliberately reaching for a flat, monotonous tone, you should try for variation in the sound of your prose.

STUDENT EXAMPLE

In this part of the world winter strips the trees early. Close to the sea, to the bay, they turn gray in late October while the ground beneath them hardens, then freezes. The sky above the outer Cape is often cloudless and blue, blue the shade of Sandwich glass. The gentle hills frost over. The birds have fled. Hidden during summer months, vistas of dune and distant houses suddenly open out, as if a swath had been cut through locust and maple and evergreen. You can see for miles. As for the wind, it's an almost constant companion, often blowing to hurricane speeds, whistling through the house, cutting under sills and window panes, with a noise like that at sea; it can drive you mad.   JANET McINTYRE

67

WRITE A STORY USING
A SMALL UNIT OF TIME

Many short stories employ a small, contained unit of time or center on a single event that provides the story with a given natural shape. For example, Nicholson Baker, in a story called "Pants on Fire," writes about putting on a shirt and taking the subway to work. Often, these stories are "short shorts" and examples can be found in Irving and Ilana Wiener Howe's anthology, *Short Shorts*, Robley Wilson's anthology from *North American Review* titled *Four Minute Fictions*, and Robert Shapard and James Thomas's *Sudden Fiction*.

THE EXERCISE

Make a list yourself of things that are done in small units of time. Here are several suggestions: Naming a pet or a child, breaking up with someone, playing a game such as Risk or Monopoly, washing a car, stealing something, waiting or standing in line for something, packing to go somewhere, cleaning a refrigerator, having a birthday party, etc.

Now write a four- to seven-page story staying within the confines of a particular time unit. For example, a birthday party story would probably last only a few hours, or an afternoon or evening; naming a pet might span a longer period of time, but will still be focused on one activity.

THE OBJECTIVE

To recognize the enormous number of shaped time units in our lives. These units can provide a natural substructure and shape for a story and make the writing of a story seem less daunting.

STUDENT EXAMPLES

One student wrote a five-page story using the time unit of changing a bicycle tire. Another student wrote a story using the time unit of wrapping Christmas presents.

A story isn't about a moment in time, a story is about *the* moment in time.

W. D. WETHERELL

68

TABOOS: WEAK ADVERBS
AND ADJECTIVES

It's been said that the adjective is the enemy of the noun and the adverb is the enemy of the verb. In *On Becoming a Novelist*, John Gardner said, "Adverbs are either the dullest tools or the sharpest in the novelist's toolbox." Adverbs are not meant to augment a verb or change it—as in *walked slowly*—but to create friction with the verb or to alter its meaning.

Pair the following adverbs with different verbs to see how they change those verbs: relentlessly, conscientiously, guiltily, chastely, uncharacteristically, reluctantly, gratuitously, erroneously, furtively, and inadequately.

Adjectives may seem to bolster nouns when in fact they often weaken them. The following are examples of adverbs and adjectives when they are used well:

> She had been to Germany, Italy, everywhere that one visits *acquistively*.
>
> ELIZABETH BOWEN, *The Last September*

> Within the parson's house death was *zealously* kept in view and lectured on.
>
> ISAK DINESEN, "Peter and Rosa"

> She jammed the pedal to the floor, and like something huge and prehistoric and pea-brained, the Jeep leapt *stupidly* out of its stall.
>
> SHARON SHEEHE STARK, *A Wrestling Season*

> I have always enjoyed gestures—never failing to bow, for example, when I finished dancing with a woman—but one attribute I have acquired with age is the ability to predict when I am about to act *foolishly*.
>
> ETHAN CANIN, *Emperor of the Air*

190

She reached again for the door and kept her eyes on him, like a captive who edges *watchfully* towards escape.

SHIRLEY HAZZARD, *The Transit of Venus*

So closely had we become tied to the river that we could sense where it lay and make for it *instinctively* like cattle.

W. D. WETHERELL, *Chekhov's Sister*

When Sula first visited the Wright house, Helene's *curdled* scorn turned to butter.

TONI MORRISON, *Sula*

With a *bladdery* whack it [the boat] slapped apart and sprang away.

SHARON SHEEHE STARK, *A Wrestling Season*

Charmian sat with her eyes closed, attempting to put her thoughts into *alphabetical* order.

MURIEL SPARK, *Memento Mori*

Hank was not accepted at Harvard Law School; but *good-hearted* Yale took him.

JOHN UPDIKE, "The Other"

THE EXERCISE

Circle all adverbs and adjectives in a published story and decide which ones work. Then, exchange all weak adverbs and adjectives for strong ones of your own. Consider omitting them altogether.

THE OBJECTIVE

To be alert to the power—and the weakness—of these verbal spices. To avoid them except when they can add something you really need.

STUDENT EXAMPLE

Hunched over, scissors clasped in her hands, the old woman passed like a shadow behind a screen of young birch and stepped *possessively* into her neighbor's garden.

COLLEEN GILLARD

The difference between the right word and the nearly right word is the same as that between lightning and the lightning bug.

MARK TWAIN

69

TRANSPORTATION: GETTING THERE ISN'T HALF THE FUN—IT'S BORING

THIS ISN'T STRICTLY AN EXERCISE: IT'S MORE OF A REMINDER. WHEN moving characters from one place to another write about how they got there only if it's crucial. Think of the movies—rarely do we see a character on a bus or in a train *unless the trip itself tells us something we absolutely need to know about the story or the character.* The lovers are in bed; next thing we see they're in a little bistro, smooching over a glass of Pernod. Who cares how they got from bed to bistro? Avoid stairs, sidewalks, subways, planes, trains, and automobiles if you can tell your story as completely without them.

70

PRACTICE WRITING GOOD, CLEAN PROSE

from Christopher Keane

Too often beginning writers think in terms of story, rather than in terms of words—of building a story with words. As a result, their early efforts are often overwritten and flowery. The following exercise will challenge your use of language—and it might change the way you write.

THE EXERCISE

Write a short story using words of only one syllable.

THE OBJECTIVE

To make you conscious of word choice.

EXAMPLE

Fire
I see her in a red dress, a red bow in her hair. She would have on black shoes and white socks. The socks would be up to her knees. She would have been, say, five years old at the time the fire broke out. It would have still been dark; it would have been cold.

She would be in her room at the time.

She would have waked from a deep sleep as if pushed or shoved. She would have known what to do. She was that way, they tell me. She was that kind of child.

I see her leave her room, stand at the top of the stairs in the front hall, smell the smoke. She would be dressed; she put on her clothes when she climbed out of bed. When she smelled smoke she would scream a fire scream that would start at the base of her throat, pass through her lips in a howl. The howl would wake those in the rest of the house. It would curl through the rooms, ride the smoke that climbed the stairs, seep through doors, cloud the glass.

The man got up first and woke his wife. They heard the child's howl filled with smoke, and they raced to the cribs of the twins, they raced to their room. Flames licked the closed doors, climbed the walls.

The man and his wife crept down the back stairs. They heard the girl's scream but there was no way to reach her. There was no time. They did not want to leave the house, but they had to. While there was still time. They must save at all cost what they had in their arms. Each held one of the twins that they took from the cribs. The twins slept on. They slept a dead sleep, safe in the arms that held them.

I see her red dress. I see a red bow in her hair. She would be told she saved them all, and she would be glad. She would have scars on her face and arms. The scars would hurt. The fire would be with her through life.

She would see the red dress and the red bow in her dreams, the white socks up to her knees. In her dreams, she would stand at the top of the stairs in the front hall. She would smell smoke and start to howl. The scars would not have come yet, nor the pain.

ANNE BRASHLER

71
ADDING TEXTURE

SOMETIMES STORIES FEEL THIN, AND YOU ARE AT A LOSS AS TO HOW to provide them with more texture. This exercise is designed to show you that early drafts of stories are quite flexible and capable of being opened up. Even when suggestions come from "outside" the story, your own imagination is still in control of selecting the material and the details to make these suggested additions an organic part of your story.

THE EXERCISE

Choose a story to work with that is still in an early draft form. Read it through so you are thoroughly familiar with it and with the characters. Then find a place in the story to complete and insert the following sentences (change the pronoun as necessary).

The last few nights she had a recurring dream (or nightmare) about _____ .

Her mother always warned her that _____ .

The one thing I couldn't say was _____ .

The telephone rang. It was a wrong number but the caller refused to hang up. Instead, she _____ . (Have at least five or six exchanges.)

Something seemed different _____ .

The last time he had worn this _____ was when _____ .

If someone said make a wish, she would wish for _____ .

Secretly, I collected _____ .

Outside, it was _____ . (Make the weather do something, for example, play off the inside atmosphere. Choose a season.)

Suddenly, she remembered she had forgotten to _____ .

On the TV (or radio or CD player) _____ was _____ .

She suspected that _____ .

The smell of _____ brought back _____ .

As a child, he had learned _____ .

Now come up with some of your own inserts.

THE OBJECTIVE

To experience how your semiconscious imagination is capable of conjuring up material that is absolutely organic to your story for each "fill-in" from the above list. Writers who do this exercise are always amazed at how something so seemingly artificial can provide them with effective additions to their stories.

STUDENT EXAMPLE

Last night Bobby had the dream again that Albert was down in the basement, he had all the bodies in the basement, everyone strapped to a chair in a big circle, and the washer was going, rumbling and ticking like there were rocks in it, and Albert was in the middle of the circle with a beer in his hand and he was singing, spinning around and singing to each body, bending, bowing to each one and Bobby yelled to him Albert what the fuck, what the fuck Albert and Albert sang to him too, sang get your own beer, get your own beer brother Bobby, and that's when he realized what the bumping noise was, it was their shoes, all of their shoes, Albert was washing their shoes in the washer, all their feet were bare, purple, and Albert was still singing to him, singing now I'm cleaning their shoes.

JIM MEZZANOTTE, "BROTHERS"

All really satisfying stories, I believe, can generally be described as spendthrift. . . . A spendthrift story has a strange way of seeming bigger than the sum of its parts; it is stuffed full; it gives a sense of possessing further information that could be divulged if called for. Even the sparest in style implies a torrent of additional details barely suppressed, bursting through the seams.

ANNE TYLER

72

NAMING THE DINER,
NAMING THE DIET, NAMING THE DOG

IN AN EARLIER EXERCISE, "NAMING YOUR CHARACTERS" (P. 42), YOU learned how to choose a character's name with care and respect for the essence of that character.

Likewise, during the course of writing stories set in counties and towns with restaurants and mortuaries, stories in which characters play in rock bands, buy race horses, play on football teams, or found new religions, you are going to have to name it all. Think of William Faulkner's Yoknapatawpha County, Thomas Hardy's Wessex, Willa Cather's Red Cloud, Marilynne Robinson's Fingerbone Lake, Anne Tyler's Homesick Restaurant and travel guide series, *The Accidental Tourist*, and Oscar Hijuelos's Mambo Kings. Names matter.

THE EXERCISE

In your notebook, keep a list of unusual names for potential characters. In fact, every writer should have a collection of old yearbooks, benefit programs, phonebooks, and so forth to browse through when he needs to name a character. And don't stop there. Keep lists for things you might need to name sometime in a story. Remember that tone is important, so when naming the following things choose an earnest name and a farcical one.

Name the following things. Imagine stories they might go in.

a desert town
a race horse
a literary magazine
a new disease

a football team
a diner
a new religion
a new planet

a rock band   a polluted river
a summer cottage   a poetry collection
triplets   a chihuahua
a liqueur   a burglar
a beauty salon   a bar
a new diet   a lipstick color
a soap opera   a yacht

THE OBJECTIVE

To loosen up your imagination by naming things you wouldn't
ordinarily have to name—never mind "own."

STUDENT EXAMPLES

Clearly, the students had more fun with the farcical names.

Desert town	
Drymouth	NOREN CACERES
Race horse	
Running Scared	CHRISTY VELADOTA
Windpasser	SAM HALPERT
Race Elements	JAY GREENBERG
Literary magazine	
Listen	GREG DUYCK
New Disease	
Afluenza	MOLLY LANZAROTTA
Rock band	
Heidi and the Alps	KARLA HORNER
Wake-up Call	GREG DUYCK
Summer cottage	
Bric-a-brac	KARLA HORNER
Triplets	
Holt, Rinehart, and Winston	ROBERT WERNER

Liqueur
Velvet Elvis   MOLLY LANZAROTTA

Beauty salon
Tressed for Success   E. J. GRAFF

Football team
Cape Cod Quahogs   ANNE DONOVAN

Diner
Crisco   DAVID ZIMMERMAN

New religion
People of the Tree   KARLA HORNER

Planet
Pica   DAWN BAKER

Polluted river
Floop River   DANIEL BIGMAN
Fever Stream   SANDY YANNONE

Poetry collection
Camphor, Floral, Mint, Musk   SARA GAMBRILL

Chihuahua
Bruno's Lunch   KAREN BROCK

Burglar
Nick Spieze   GREG DUYCK

Bar
Recovery Room   SUSAN GANLEY

Diet
Body Carpenter   DAVID ZIMMERMAN
The Remote Control Diet   SANDY YANNONE

Soap opera
On Borrowed Time   JAY GREENBERG
The Rammed and the Damned (on cable T.V.)
                                                SANFORD GOLDEN

Lipstick
Screaming Salsa   EVE BAKER
Sanddollar Taupe   PATRICIA FITZGERALD

Yacht
Waves Goodbye   MOLLY LANZAROTTA

73

CUTTING TO THE BONE

from David Ray

Wᴴᴇɴ Hᴇᴍɪɴɢᴡᴀʏ ᴡᴀꜱ ᴀꜱᴋᴇᴅ ɪꜰ ʜᴇ ʀᴇᴠɪꜱᴇᴅ ᴍᴜᴄʜ, ʜᴇ ᴀɴꜱᴡᴇʀᴇᴅ by handing across a story and telling his interviewer to take it home and read it carefully and tell him the next day if he had found a single word that could be cut. The interviewer decided that this was Hemingway's way of telling him that the story had undergone many revisions.

THE EXERCISE

Take a passage of your work and read through it at least three times, questioning every word. Then cross out every word possible. The adverbs will, no doubt, be the first to go, then most adjectives. See if prepositional phrases can be omitted or replaced by a single word. Is description excessive? Ask if a word, a sentence, a paragraph, or even a page can be cut.

THE OBJECTIVE

To make the writing as spare and trim and essential as Hemingway's or Chekhov's. Recall Chekhov's advice about spare description, "very brief and relevant ... one ought to seize upon the little particulars, grouping them in such a way that, in reading, when you shut your eyes, you get a picture." He regarded it as an insult to overdescribe; the writer gives just enough detail to evoke the reader's knowledge of life. He also suggested, of course, that one write a beginning, middle, and end, then cut the beginning and the end. The story is what's left. It is remarkable how often that advice is just what is needed. The challenge to every word will make the writer aware of her tolerance for fat!

XI: GAMES

W E HAVE INCLUDED THREE GAMES WITH WORDS PARTLY FOR YOUR amusement and partly as a demonstration that the combination and recombination of the twenty-six letters of the alphabet don't always have to end in so-called deathless prose. Words are magical playthings as well as instruments of persuasion, entertainment, enlightenment, social change, and uplift. These games are more fun than going to the movies, watching television, or playing poker.

205

74

LEARNING TO LIE

Beginning writers often resist their imaginations as something childish, exotic, or out of reach when in fact everyone has at some time told a lie. So for this exercise think of writing fiction as telling a lie. (This exercise is actually a variation on a late-night parlor game and is particularly good for the first session of a class or workshop.)

THE EXERCISE

In two or three sentences, write down three unusual, startling, or amusing things you did or that happened to you. One thing must be true, the other two must be lies. Use details.

Here is what one writer used for herself.

> Elvis Presley wrote me a two-sentence letter after I sent him a poem I'd written about him and a picture of my younger sister in a bikini.

> The first time I heard him play, Buddy Rich threw me a drum stick during a drum roll and never missed a beat.

> I asked Mick Jagger to sign a program for me, but he said he'd prefer to sign my left white shoe. And he did.

Now everybody do one.

Then one by one read them to the group. The group is allowed to ask questions pertaining specifically to the details. For example, someone might ask the above person, "Why did you send your sister's photograph instead of your own?" Or "What was Buddy Rich playing?" Or "Do you still have your shoe and if so, where is it?" The "author" has to be able to

think on her feet, to make up more convincing details, to "lie."
Then ask for a vote as to which story is true and which stories
are fictions. It is surprising how many people are already good
storytellers, capable of finding the concrete persuasive detail.
(The second "lie" is true.)

THE OBJECTIVE

To understand how we can exaggerate events in our lives, appropriate the lives of others—friends, enemies, strangers—or
just plain out-and-out lie. All these are ways of using what we
see and experience to produce fiction.

STUDENT EXAMPLE

I once stole a pair of diamond earrings from Saks Fifth Ave.
After I found out they were cubic zirconia, I took them back
and slipped them into the display counter. Why get in trouble
for *faux* anything?

I have tried to get my cat, Frosty, on David Letterman's
Stupid Pet Tricks for the past three years. I've gotten into the
semifinals, only to have Frosty pee all over everyone who tried
to coax her into doing her tricks.

When I was young, I was convinced that my two older
brothers were plotting to kill my mother. I remember it so
vividly that I still can't eat Christmas dinner without worry-
ing about the carving knives.

(The third "lie" is true.)   CLAIRE ISRAEL

75

THE DICTIONARY GAME

IN ONE SENSE, ALL FICTION WRITING IS ARTIFICE: DIALOGUE ISN'T LIKE real speech; stories are, for the most part, invented; singing prose is as carefully crafted as a glass bowl. The following calls on you to exercise pure inventiveness, pure craft.

THE EXERCISE

A game for four to six players. Using a standard English dictionary, each player takes turns being *it*. The *it* finds a word that none of the other players knows the meaning of (everyone is on his honor to tell the truth about this). The *it* then writes down the real definition, while the other players invent and write down a definition they hope will be construed as the real one. They then pass their papers in to the *it*, who gives each definition a number, making sure they are all legible. The *it* reads each one in turn. The players make up their minds about which definition is real and then they vote by holding up the number of fingers corresponding to the number of the definition they choose. You may not vote for your own definition. Scoring: You get one point for each player who thinks yours is the correct definition. If you guess the real definition you get one point. If no one guesses the real definition, the *it* gets one point.

THE OBJECTIVE

Words are what it's all about. You can play around with them in much the same way you play around with plot and with ideas.

76

FICTIONARY:
A VARIATION OF DICTIONARY

It can be fun to try to invent sentences that another writer might have written. This game is played using the books of writers who are fairly well known to all the players—say books by Philip Roth, Henry James, Virginia Woolf, Saul Bellow, Bobbie Ann Mason, Isaac Bashevis Singer, etc. Choose writers with a very distinct style.

THE EXERCISE

Choose one sentence, preferably one with four to ten words, from a story or a novel. Next, call out the first letter for each word in the sentence. For example, if you were to use this sentence from John Gardner's *Grendel*, "Pick an apocalypse, any apocalypse," you would call out P A A A A. Then ask the players to make up a sentence containing words beginning with those letters. After that, the same rules apply as those for Dictionary (see page 209).

THE OBJECTIVE

To have fun with language and try to imitate or outwrite the published author.

XII: LEARNING FROM THE GREATS

> The great guides were the books I discovered in the Johns
> Hopkins library, where my student job was to file books away.
> One was more or less encouraged to take a cart of books and
> go back into the stacks and not come out for seven or eight
> hours. So I read what I was filing. My great teachers (the best
> thing that can happen to a writer) were Scheherazade, Homer,
> Virgil, and Boccaccio; also the great Sanskrit taletellers. I was
> impressed forever with the width as well as the depth of lit-
> erature—
>
> —JOHN BARTH

WE HOPE THIS BOOK WILL TAKE YOU IN TWO DIRECTIONS: FIRST,
into your own well of inspiration, your own store of forgotten
or overlooked material, and into your own writing and, second, back to the greats who are your true teachers.

F. Scott Fitzgerald is one of these teachers, and he names
his own teachers in the following passage.

> By style, I mean color. . . . I want to be able to do anything
> with words: handle slashing, flaming descriptions like Wells,
> and use the paradox with the clarity of Samuel Butler, the
> breadth of Bernard Shaw and the wit of Oscar Wilde, I want
> to do the wide sultry heavens of Conrad, the rolled gold sun-
> downs and crazy-quilt skies of Hichens and Kipling as well as
> the pastelle [sic] dawns and twilights of Chesterton. All that

is by way of example. As a matter of fact I am a professional literary thief, hot after the best methods of every writer in my generation.

In a letter Fitzgerald again talks of how he has learned something. He says, "the motif of the 'dying fall' [in *Tender is the Night*] was absolutely deliberate and did not come from the diminution of vitality but from a definite plan. That particular trick is one that Ernest Hemingway and I worked out—probably from Conrad's preface to *The Nigger* [*of the Narcissus*]." Madison Smartt Bell echoes this sense of learning tricks from a master in his dedication for *The Washington Square Ensemble.* He says, "This book is dedicated to the long patience of my parents with a tip of the trick hat to George Garrett."

The exercises in this next section are meant to show you how to read for inspiration and instruction. Study the letters and journals of writers to discover how they grappled with problems you will encounter in your own fiction. For example, Flaubert worried about the "lack of action" in *Madame Bovary.* In a letter to Louise Colet he says, "The psychological development of my characters is giving me a lot of trouble; and everything, in this novel, depends on it." And he immediately comes up with the solution, "for in my opinion, ideas can be as entertaining as actions, but in order to be so they must flow one from the other like a series of cascades, carrying the reader along midst the throbbing of sentences and the seething of metaphors."

And read what writers say about writing, for example John Barth's *Lost in the Funhouse,* Elizabeth Bowen's *Collected Impressions,* Ray Carver's *Fires,* Annie Dillard's *Living by Fiction* and *The Writing Life,* John Gardner's *The Art of Fiction* and *Becoming a Novelist,* E. M. Forster's *Aspects of the Novel,* William Gass's *On Being Blue,* Henry James's prefaces to his novels, Flannery O'Connor's *Mystery and Manners,* Eudora Welty's *The Eye of the Story,* and Virginia Woolf's *A Room of One's Own,* among others. And now on to our exercises for learning from the greats.

77

FINDING INSPIRATION IN OTHER SOURCES—POETRY, NONFICTION, ETC.

A WRITER IS SOMEONE WHO READS. WE RECOMMEND THAT YOU READ the letters and notebooks of writers, biographies and autobiographies, plays and poetry, history and religion. Reading for writers has always engendered a cross-pollination of ideas and forms. For the writer, everything is a possible source for an epigraph, a title, a story, a novel.

Below are some well-chosen epigraphs.

CHARLES BAXTER, *First Light*
Life can only be understood backwards; but it must be lived forwards.
SØREN KIERKEGAARD

F. SCOTT FITZGERALD, *The Great Gatsby*
Then wear the gold hat, if that will move her;
    If you can bounce high, bounce for her too,
Till she cry "Lover, gold-hatted, high-bouncing lover,
    I must have you!"
THOMAS PARKE D'INVILLIERS

JOHN HAWKES, *The Blood Oranges*
Is there then any terrestrial paradise where, amidst the whispering of the olive-leaves, people can be with whom they like and have what they like and take their ease in shadows and in coolness?
FORD MADOX FORD, *The Good Soldier*

NADINE GORDIMER, *Burger's Daughter*
I am the place in which something has occurred.
CLAUDE LÉVI-STRAUSS

213

AMY HEMPEL, *Reasons to Live*
Because grief unites us,
like the locked antlers of moose
who die on their knees in pairs.

WILLIAM MATTHEWS

JOYCE CAROL OATES, *Them*
. . . because we are poor
Shall we be vicious?

JOHN WEBSTER, *The White Devil*

SHARON SHEEHE STARK, *A Wrestling Season*
Life's nonsense pierces us with strange relation.

WALLACE STEVENS

THE EXERCISE

Read widely for inspiration and then use an original text as
an epigraph for your own story or novel. For example, think
of Stanley Kunitz's wonderful line: "The thing that eats the
heart is mostly heart." This would make a superb epigraph to
a story, collection, or novel titled "Mostly Heart." Begin a story
with this line in mind. Or write a story that illustrates this line
from John le Carré's *Tinker, Tailor, Soldier, Spy:* "There are
moments that are made up of too much stuff for them to be
lived at the time they occur."

Choose several of your favorite poems and reread them with
an eye toward finding a title or using a line as an epigraph to
a story. Or choose a sentence from an essay or popular song.

Read, read, read. Then write, write, write. Sometimes in
reverse order.

THE OBJECTIVE

To absorb what we read in a way that allows it to spark our own creativity, to use it as inspiration for our own writing. To build on what has gone before.

Mary McCarthy once lost the only manuscript copy of a novel. Interviewer Bob Cromie said to her, "But it's your novel, you can write it again." McCarthy replied, "Oh, I couldn't do that—I know how it ends."

78

PLACES WITHOUT PEOPLE

VERY FEW GOOD SHORT STORIES OR NOVELS FLOAT IN TIME AND SPACE; they are firmly anchored in a particular year, or years, and in a singular place—whether it's a rooming house, region, or country. Place matters. You can't for example, imagine *The Catcher in the Rye* taking place in third-century Rome or even the American Southwest at the beginning of the twentieth century. It must be post–World War II New York. Place is thematically almost as important as characters or plot.

THE EXERCISE

Look at the work of the following authors and try to analyze how they managed to give their settings so much power and personality: William Faulkner (a mythical Southern county), Nathaniel Hawthorne (a severe New England town), Herman Melville (the sea and ships), Evelyn Waugh (London), John Cheever (suburbia), Toni Cade Bambara (Atlanta), and Jay McInerney (New York City). These are just a few authors among many who recognize that characters must not float in space but be anchored to a particular place in a particular time.

THE OBJECTIVE

To learn that setting and place are crucial elements in narrative. Where you set your story has to reflect—or create tension with—the overall theme and plot of the work.

79

THE SKY'S THE LIMIT: HOMAGE TO KAFKA AND GARCÍA MÁRQUEZ

from Christopher Noël

In a *Paris Review* interview, Gabriel García Márquez says,

At the university in Bogotá, I started making new friends and acquaintances, who introduced me to contemporary writers. One night a friend lent me a book of short stories by Franz Kafka. I went back to the pension where I was staying and began to read *The Metamorphosis*. The first line almost knocked me off the bed. I was so surprised. The first line reads, 'As Gregor Samsa awoke that morning from uneasy dreams, he found himself transformed in his bed into a gigantic insect . . .' When I read the line I thought to myself that I didn't know anyone was allowed to write things like that. If I had known, I would have started writing a long time ago. So I immediately started writing.

THE EXERCISE

For inspiration read Kafka's story, or perhaps García Márquez's "A Very Old Man with Enormous Wings." Then if you are part of a group, each member should write a fantastical first line and then pass it to the left (or right). Each person, receiving a first line from her neighbor should then try to make good on its implicit riches, to open up a world from this seed, one that is different from the everyday world but nonetheless full of concrete detail and clear and consistent qualities, rules of being.

THE OBJECTIVE

To loosen up your thinking, to countenance a greater range of possibilities and to see that sometimes even the most apparently frivolous or ludicrous notions, completely implausible even for the slanted implausibility that writers use, can turn out to be just the ticket. What's strange can be made to seem necessary in a story; you can work to solidify the strangeness if, while you're writing, you keep a sort of grim faith at those pivotal moments—whether the first line or the third chapter or the final paragraph—when it seems you are betraying or trivializing your authentic vision of the world.

STUDENT EXAMPLES

I scream each time I see that the house is surrounded, and I know this makes Carmen's patience wavery, like the heat mirages. Carmen has always lived in this desert and tells me that it is the normal way for Joshua trees to behave. But how am I to get used to them, all standing there with their arms raised each time I pass the window and forget not to look out. The Joshua trees are moving closer every day, and to me this is ominous, Carmen or no Carmen.

This house, this desert, are supposed to be for my health. Carmen, too, is supposed to be for my health. The doctor in Boston told my son so. Warm climate, a companion, and the old lady will be all set. Well, that doctor didn't know about the ways of the desert. I watch as the Joshua trees group and regroup like some stunted army, never quite making up their minds that they are going to advance. Bradford gets upset on the phone if I talk about the Joshua trees, how they are preparing for some sort of final march. Carmen can see it in the moon, although I don't tell Bradford this lest he think Carmen a bad influence.

MOLLY LANZAROTTA, "Running with the Joshua Tree"

When Rene returned from the army, I felt at first that we should not contradict him, although the letter that had come weeks before clearly stated he was dead.

And sure enough, my cousin Rene did not at all wish to discuss the manner of his dying, which had been described in great detail in the letter from his friend in the army, how he had been dismembered by the rebels in the mountains, how he'd been skinned and scalped, his eyes gouged out and any number of things, to the point that there was nothing left to send home of him, nothing for us to mourn but the letter. I

218

was practiced at this, this sudden grief with no ceremony, and wondered whether soon I would be the last one of this family, too, just one young girl left from so many.

And then Rene wandered in on a night that was gray with the glow of distant explosions, gray himself, covered with the dirt of the mountains and the dust of the desert our town has become. Little Yolanda shrieked when he pulled back the burlap we'd hung over the door of our collapsing home, and, of course, none of us could finish our meal. Rene sat down and ate everything on each of our plates, while his brother Evelio shouted, paced the room and questioned him, and his mother, Luisa, wept and kissed him and pulled on her rosary until it snapped, showering us all with tiny black beads. It seemed that they had cut the voice out of Rene as well, when they killed him, because he did not want to talk at all.

MOLLY LANZAROTTA, "The Death of Rene Paz"

If it hadn't been for my long serpentine tail, I wouldn't have lost my job as a cabdriver. It wasn't that management objected so much, God knows good help is hard to find these days, but eventually passengers complained, especially when I became agitated, say, in heavy traffic and whipped my tail into the backseat. I even struck a passenger once, but not on purpose or forcefully, and no permanent damage was done. I apologized afterward. I didn't get many tips.

I tried to make a virtue of my tail by decorating it on holidays, tying bright ribbons around its circumference until it looked like a barber pole, or the lance of a medieval knight. Things seemed to be working, at least until that incident with the motorcycle cop.

"Believe me, Melvin, it's not you," the dispatcher said. "Well, actually, it is you, in a way. But it's not personal," he pleaded, larding his voice with concern to avoid a class action suit. "Insurance is eating me up, man. That pedestrian you hit the other day . . ."

"I can explain that. I was giving a left turn signal . . ."

"Melvin, go to a doctor. Get it taken off. You're a good driver. You got a future."

"But it's part of me. It kind of gives me something to lean against."

He shrugged his shoulders toward the picture of the near-naked woman embracing a tire on the Parts Pups calendar on

the wall. "He likes it," he said, as if to her. Then he looked at me. "Okay, Mel, you like it. You live with it. But not here."
And so I was out of a job.

GENE LANGSTON, "Fired"

I read Shakespeare *directly* I have finished writing. When my mind is agape and redhot. Then it is astonishing. I never yet knew how amazing his stretch and speed and word coining power is, until I felt it utterly outpace and outrace my own, seeming to start equal and then I see him draw ahead and to things I could not in my wildest tumult and utmost press of mind imagine.

VIRGINIA WOOLF, *A Writer's Diary*

80

LEARNING FROM
THE GREATS

Most writers can look back and name the books that seemed to fling open doors for them, books that made them want to go to the typewriter and begin to write one word after another.

When asked if one writer had influenced her more than others, Joan Didion replied,

> I always say Hemingway, because he taught me how sentences worked. When I was fifteen or sixteen I would type out his stories to learn how sentences worked. . . . A few years ago when I was teaching a course at Berkeley I reread *A Farewell to Arms* and fell right back into those sentences. I mean they're perfect sentences. Very direct sentences, smooth rivers, clear water over granite, no sinkholes.

THE EXERCISE

Choose a writer you admire, one who has withstood the test of time. Type out that writer's stories or several chapters from a novel. Try to analyze how the sentences work, how their vocabulary differs from your own, how the structure of the story emerges from the language, how the writer intersperses scene with narrative summary. Feel in your fingers what is different about that prose.

THE OBJECTIVE

To understand how another writer's sentences work. To learn to analyze what succeeds in the fiction of a master and *how* it succeeds.

81

IMITATION: SINCERE FLATTERY—
AND LEARNING

Oɴᴄᴇ ʏᴏᴜ ʜᴀᴠᴇ ᴛʏᴘᴇᴅ ᴏᴜᴛ ᴛʜᴇ ᴡᴏʀᴅs, sᴇɴᴛᴇɴᴄᴇs, ᴀɴᴅ ᴘᴀʀᴀ-
graphs of other writers, you will know a lot more about the
way their prose works. So why not put this knowledge to use
and actually try to imitate them—not in your own stories but
in their stories.

THE EXERCISE

In a story or novel by a writer you admire, find a place between two sentences that seems like a "crack" that could be
"opened up." Next, write your own paragraph or scene and
insert it into this place. Now read the entire story including
your addition.

THE OBJECTIVE

To understand just how much you need to know to really understand another person's story and how it works—and then
add to it. The answer: everything—characterization, plot, tone,
style, etc.

STUDENT EXAMPLES

Two consecutive sentences from "A Very Old Man with Enormous Wings," by Gabriel García Márquez:

> The Angel was no less stand-offish with him than with other
> mortals, but he tolerated the most ingenious infamies with
> the patience of a dog who had no illusions. They both came
> down with chicken pox at the same time.

Two students inserted the following additions between the above two sentences.

The child would build, over days, leaning castles of shells and stray sections of wire against the Angel's unmoving body. Mornings after the old man had shifted during sleep, the child would run out of the hot house, sweating already, to scream at him. The child had not learned the patterns of the old man, his times of stillness and the moments of earthquake movement that bent the chicken coop wire.

Pelayo would take the child fishing every week. After these trips, the two would walk up to the chicken coop with their string of catch and hold them up for the Angel. But he would not turn and look at them and Pelayo came to doubt the Angel's sailor origins. The wise neighbor told Pelayo and Elisenda that the child would be an altar boy if only he kept a safe distance from the Angel, however, the child continued to play in the chicken coop, and began to call the old man the hen-man.

Greg Duyck

The child hung dried crabs and lizards off the fallen Angel's wings, climbed onto his back to grasp the crow feathers in his tiny hands. The child tried to pull the enormous wing wide, imagining they were flying as the chickens ticked his muddy toes. He thought of the Angel as a great, broken doll and spent hours tying colored rags around his dried fig of a head, hanging rosaries around his neck and painting the crevices of his face with soot and red earth, the Angel all the while mumbling in his befuddled sailor's dialect.

When the wise neighbor woman heard words of the Angel's language coming out of the child's mouth, she shook her head and threw more mothballs into the chicken coop. She told Elisenda, "Your child will grow wings or be carried off. He will disappear into the heavens." For a while, Elisenda tried to keep the child in the garden and Pelayo repaired the broken wires of the chicken coop. But the child continued to play on the other side of the wire and the Angel remained so inert that Elisenda ceased to believe it was the Angel's tongue her child spoke at all, but his own made up child's language. Soon the child was once again playing inside the coop, flying on the back of the old man.

Molly Lanzarotta

Two consecutive sentences from *Lost in the Funhouse*, by John Barth:

Ambrose's former archenemy.
Shortly after the mirror room he'd groped along a musty corridor, his heart already misgiving him at the absence of phosphorescent arrows and other signs.

One student inserted this between the above two sentences.

Ambrose wanders aimlessly, loses sight of Peter as Magda chases him beyond the mirrors, into the darkness of the next room. Their laughter echos and he cannot tell the direction from which it comes. He will not call out to them. He is not lost yet. He will find his way out on his own. The smudges of hand prints on the mirrors reassure Ambrose that he is not the only one to follow this path through the funhouse. In one of the reflections, his arm is around the waist of an exquisite young woman with a figure unusually well developed for her age. He is taller, wearing a sailor's uniform. The image moves away, but Ambrose remains. Glass. *Not a mirror.* Sentence fragments can be used to emphasize discoveries or thoughts that suddenly occur to a character. The point is communicated to the reader without saying "he thought . . ." The fragmented thought may be used in combination with italics to create a feeling of urgency. Ambrose tries creating a path parallel to the one taken by the others but is constantly forced to change direction as the mirrors obscure his goal. At an unordained moment he reaches out to touch what he thinks is another mirror, but turns out in fact to be a passageway.

ZAREH ARTINIAN

82

BORROWING CHARACTERS

Authors have been borrowing characters from other authors' works for years. Some well known examples are Jean Rhys's wonderful novel *Wide Sargasso Sea*, which provides an account of the early life of Mrs. Rochester, the wife of Mr. Rochester in Charlotte Brontë's *Jane Eyre*. George Macdonald Fraser uses Tom Brown and Flashman from Thomas Hughes's novel, *Tom Brown's School Days*. And there have been any number of continuations of the adventures of Sherlock Holmes. Nicholas Meyer's *The Seven Percent Solution* and Rick Boyer's *The Giant Rat of Sumatra* are two of the best. John Gardner wrote a novel titled *Grendel* about the beast in *Beowulf*. Joseph Heller brought King David once again to life in *God Knows*.

THE EXERCISE

Take an antagonist or a minor character from a story or novel by someone else—a character who has always intrigued you. Make that person the protagonist in a scene or story of your own. For example, what would Allie Fox's wife say if she were to tell her version of *Mosquito Coast*, or write a story about their courtship? And what would Rabbit's illegitimate daughter, from Updike's *Rabbit* novels, say if she could tell her story?

THE OBJECTIVE

To enter into the imaginative world of another writer, to understand that particular world, and to build from it.

83

WHAT KEEPS YOU READING?

In *THE EYE OF THE STORY*, EUDORA WELTY WRITES, "LEARNING TO write may be part of learning to read. For all I know, writing comes out of a superior devotion to reading."

Part of the apprenticeship of being a successful writer is learning to read like a writer, discovering how a particular story catches your attention and keeps you involved right straight through to the end.

THE EXERCISE

Halfway through a story ask yourself several questions: What do I care about? What has been set in motion that I want to see completed? Where is the writer taking me? Then finish reading the story and see how well the writer met the expectations that she raised for you.

THE OBJECTIVE

To illustrate how the best stories and novels set up situations that are resolved by the time you finish the story or close the book. To learn how to arouse the reader's curiosity or create expectations in the first half of your story or novel, and then to decide to what degree you should feel obliged to meet those expectations.

SELECTED BIBLIOGRAPHY

BORGES, JORGE LUIS. 1973. *Borges on Writing.* Ed. Norman Thomas di Giovanni, Daniel Halpern, and Frank MacShane. New York: E. P. Dutton.

BOWEN, ELIZABETH. 1950. *Collected Impressions.* New York: Alfred A. Knopf.

BRANDE, DOROTHEA. 1981. *On Becoming a Writer.* Los Angeles: Jeremy Tarcher.

BURROWAY, JANET. 1982. *Writing Fiction.* Boston: Little, Brown.

FITZGERALD, F. SCOTT. 1978. *The Notebooks of F. Scott Fitzgerald.* Ed. Matthew J. Bruccoli. New York: Harcourt Brace Jovanovich.

FORSTER, E. M. 1954. *Aspects of the Novel.* New York: Harcourt Brace & World.

GARDNER, JOHN. 1984. *The Art of Fiction.* New York: Alfred A. Knopf.

HALL, DONALD. 1979. *Writing Well.* Boston: Little, Brown.

HEMINGWAY, ERNEST. 1984. *Ernest Hemingway on Writing.* Ed. Larry W. Phillips. New York: Charles Scribner's Sons.

HILLS, RUST. 1977. *Writing in General and the Short Story in Particular.* Boston: Houghton Mifflin.

HUGO, RICHARD. 1979. *The Triggering Town.* New York: W. W. Norton.

JAMES, HENRY. 1947. *The Art of the Novel.* Oxford: Oxford University Press.

———. 1947. *The Notebooks of Henry James.* Oxford: Oxford University Press.

———. 1948. *The Art of Fiction.* New York: Charles Scribner's Sons.

O'CONNOR, FLANNERY. 1969. *Mystery and Manners.* New York: Farrar, Straus & Giroux.

O'CONNOR, FRANK. 1963. *The Lonely Voice: A Study of the Short Story.* Cleveland: World Publishing.

PLIMPTON, GEORGE. 1953–1989. *Writers at Work: The Paris Review Interviews,* 8 vols., New York: Viking Penguin.

———. 1989. *The Writer's Chapbook.* New York: Viking.

REED, KIT. 1982. *Story First. The Writer as Insider:* Englewood Cliffs, N.J.Prentice-Hall.

WELTY, EUDORA. 1977. *The Eye of the Story.* New York: Random House.

ABOUT THE CONTRIBUTORS

PERRY GLASSER is the author of two collections of short fiction, *Suspicious Origins*, and *Singing on the Titanic*. He has taught at Drake University in Iowa and Bradford College in Vermont.

CHRISTOPHER KEANE's forthcoming novel is titled *Christmas Babies*. He is currently writing a screenplay, *The Venus Coalition*, for actor Anthony Quinn, and he teaches a graduate workshop at Emerson College in Boston.

WILLIAM MELVIN KELLEY has published four novels, including the recently reissued *A Different Drummer*, and a book of stories titled *Dancers on the Shore*. He teaches at Sarah Lawrence.

WILLIAM KITTREDGE is the author of a forthcoming autobiographical book titled *Hole in the Sky* and two previous books, *Owning It All* and *We Are Not in This Together*. He teaches at the University of Montana.

RHODA LERMAN has published five novels, the latest of which is *God's Ear*. She has been awarded an National Endowment of the Arts fellowship and is currently teaching at the State University of New York at Buffalo.

ELIZABETH LIBBEY has published two volumes of poetry: *The Crowd Inside* and *Songs of a Returning Soul*. She teaches writing workshops at Trinity College in Hartford, Connecticut.

ALISON LURIE is the author of eight novels, the latest of which is *The Truth About Lorin Jones*. Her most recent book is *Don't Tell the Grown-Ups: Subversive Children's Literature*. She is the Frederic J. Whiton Professor of American Studies at Cornell.

ROBIE MACAULEY is the author of two novels, a collection of short stories, and two nonfiction books. His *Technique in Fiction* (with George Lanning) has been reissued by St. Martin's Press.

ALEXANDRA MARSHALL is a Boston writer whose novels include *Gus in Bronze, Tender Offer,* and *The Brass Bed.* Her work in progress is titled *Child Widow.* She is a writer-in-residence at Emerson College, Boston.

CHRISTOPHER NOËL published his first novel, *Hazard and the Five Delights,* in 1988 and has a collection of stories, *The Grasshopper Girl,* forthcoming. He teaches in the Vermont College Master's of Fine Arts program in Montpelier.

JOY NOLAN is a free-lance writer of radio scripts for station WQXR in New York and is currently completing her first book of stories, *Hot Water Street.* She lives in Williamsburg, Massachusetts, and teaches at the Amherst School of the Arts.

DAVID RAY'S most recent books are *Not Far from the River* and *The Maharani's New Wall and Other Poems. Sam's Book* won the Maurice English Poetry Award in 1988. He is a professor of English at the University of Missouri-Kansas City where he teaches both fiction and poetry workshops.

LORE SEGAL'S best-known novel is *Her First American.* She is also the author of a book of Bible translations, *The Book of Adam to Moses,* and a new children's book, *Mrs. Lovewright and Purrless Her Cat.* She teaches at the Chicago Circle Campus of the University of Illinois.

THALIA SELZ has contributed fiction to many magazines, including *Partisan Review, Antaeus, Chicago,* and *New Letters.* Her stories have been anthologized in *Best American Short Stories* and *O. Henry Prize Stories.* She has won twenty-three literary prizes and fellowships. She teaches at Trinity College in Hartford, Connecticut.

SHARON SHEEHE STARK has published two books of fiction, *The Dealer's Yard and Other Stories* and *A Wrestling Season.* She is a contributor to the *Atlantic,* a recipient of Guggenheim and National Endowment of the Arts fellowships, and is on the faculty of the Vermont College Master's of Fine Arts program in Montpelier.